# THE PADARN AND PENRHYN RAILWAYS

## UNIFORM WITH THIS BOOK

Graham S. Hudson, *The Aberford Railway and the History of the Garforth Collieries*
John Thomas, *The Callander & Oban Railway*
Rex Christiansen and R. W. Miller, *The Cambrian Railways: Volume 1: 1852–1888, Volume 2: 1889–1968*
N. S. C. Macmillan, *The Campbeltown & Machrihanish Light Railway*
Patrick J. Flanagan, *The Cavan & Leitrim Railway*
Peter E. Baughan, *The Chester & Holyhead Railway, Volume 1*
Peter E. Baughan, *The Railways of Wharfedale*
Edward M. Patterson, *The Clogher Valley Railway*
Edward M. Patterson, *A History of the Narrow-gauge Railways of North East Ireland*
  Part One: *The Ballycastle Railway*
  Part Two: *The Ballymena Lines*
Edward M. Patterson, *A History of the Narrow-gauge Railways of North West Ireland*
  Part One: *The County Donegal Railways (second edition)*
  Part Two: *The Londonderry & Lough Swilly Railway*
W. E. Shepherd, *The Dublin & South Eastern Railway*
H. A. Vallance, *The Great North of Scotland Railway*
H. A. Vallance, *The Highland Railway*
H. W. Paar, *A History of the Railways of the Forest of Dean*
  Part One: *The Severn & Wye Railway*
  Part Two: *The Great Western Railway in Dean*
K. Hoole (editor), *The Hull & Barnsley Railway, Volume 1*
John Marshall, *The Lancashire & Yorkshire Railways, Volumes 1, 2 and 3*
David L. Smith, *The Little Railways of South West Scotland*
R. A. Williams, *The London & South Western Railway, Volumes 1 and 2*
D. W. Ronald and R. J. Carter, *The Longmoor Military Railway*
G. A. Brown, J. D. C. A. Prideaux and H. G. Radcliffe, *The Lynton & Barnstaple Railway*
Colin G. Maggs, *The Midland & South Western Junction Railway*
John Thomas, *The North British Railway, Volume 1*
Rex Christiansen and R. W. Miller, *The North Staffordshire Railway*
J. R. L. Currie, *The Northern Counties Railway, Volume 1, 1845–1903, Volume 2, 1903–1972*
G. Whittle, *The Railways of Consett and North West Durham*
W. J. K. Davies, *The Ravenglass & Eskdale Railway*
A. D. Farr, *The Royal Deeside Line*
Keith Turner, *The Snowdon Mountain Railway*
Robin Atthill and O. S. Nock, *The Somerset & Dorset Railway*
John Thomas, *The West Highland Railway*
H. Fayle and A. T. Newham, *The Waterford & Tramore Railway*
Ralph Cartwright and R. T. Russell, *The Welshpool & Llanfair Light Railway*

# THE PADARN AND PENRHYN RAILWAYS

and their associated systems

by
SUSAN TURNER

DAVID & CHARLES : NEWTON ABBOT
LONDON   VANCOUVER   NORTH POMFRET (VT)

0 7153 6547 9

© Susan Turner 1975
For my parents

All rights reserved. No part of this
publication may be reproduced, stored
in a retrieval system, or transmitted,
in any form or by any means, electronic,
mechanical, photocopying, recording or
otherwise, without the prior permission
of David & Charles (Holdings) Limited

Set in 11/13pt Pilgrim and printed in Great Britain
by John Sherratt & Sons Ltd
for David & Charles (Holdings) Limited
South Devon House Newton Abbot Devon

Published in the United States of America
by David and Charles Inc North Pomfret
Vermont 05053 USA

Published in Canada by Douglas David & Charles Limited
3645 McKechnie Drive West Vancouver BC

## Contents

| | | Page |
|---|---|---|
| | LIST OF ILLUSTRATIONS | 7 |
| | ACKNOWLEDGEMENTS | 10 |
| 1 | THE FORMATIVE YEARS | 11 |

Background to the slate industry - the Penrhyn estate - birth of the Penrhyn Quarry - the Vaynol estate - the rise of the Dinorwic Quarry - the Dinorwic Quarry Co - early means of transport

2 THE QUARRIES    26

The slate - sizes and prices - working in the quarries - visitors - Dinorwic tramroads - Penrhyn tramroads

3 THE PENRHYN RAILWAY    40

The Penrhyn Tramroad - Penrhyn Quarry - permanent way - a new line - the route described - Port Penrhyn - the Port Penrhyn branch - working - quarry and railway - closure

4 THE PADARN RAILWAY    65

The Dinorwic Tramroad - Dinorwic Quarry - a new line is built - the route described - years of prosperity - and dispute - two royal visits - Port Dinorwic - the Port Dinorwic incline - the Port Dinorwic branch - working - later years - closure & lifting - Marchlyn Quarry - the auctions

5 PENRHYN STOCK    99

Main line locomotives - de Wintons - Port class - Small class - Large class - others - internal combustion - passenger stock - goods stock

| | | |
|---|---|---|
| 6 | PADARN STOCK AND WORKING<br>Workmen's transport - working - accidents - locomotives - passenger stock - goods stock - velocipedes | 119 |
| 7 | DINORWIC STOCK<br>Locomotives - Mills class - Port class - Alice class - others - internal combustion - rolling stock | 145 |
| 8 | TODAY<br>The Llanberis Lake Railway - the North Wales Quarrying Museum - preserved locomotives - other preserved items - tramroads, railways and ports | 162 |

APPPENDICES

| | | |
|---|---|---|
| 1 | Chronology | 173 |
| 2 | Padarn Railway locomotive stock list | 176 |
| 3 | Padarn Railway steam: comparative dimensions | 176 |
| 4 | Dinorwic steam stock list | 177 |
| 5 | Dinorwic Hunslets: comparative dimensions | 179 |
| 6 | Dinorwic internal combustion stock list | 180 |
| 7 | Penrhyn Railway locomotive stock list | 181 |
| 8 | Penrhyn (port & quarry) steam stock list | 182 |
| 9 | Penrhyn Hunslets: comparative dimensions | 184 |
| 10 | Penrhyn internal combustion stock list | 185 |

| | |
|---|---|
| BIBLIOGRAPHY | 187 |
| INDEX | 189 |

# List of Illustrations

### PLATES

| | Page |
|---|---|
| Course of the Dinorwic Village Tramway (B. J. Williams) | 33 |
| The Deiniolen inclines on the Dinorwic Tramroad (B. J. Williams) | 33 |
| Penrhyn Tramroad - former course at the Dinas incline (Locomotive & General Railway Photographs) | 34 |
| Penrhyn Tramroad - former course at Llandegai (K. Turner) | 34 |
| On the Padarn - slate train at Penllyn (L & GRP) | 51 |
| On the Padarn - train at Bethel (L & GRP) | 51 |
| Padarn signal (L & GRP) | 52 |
| Waggons at Penscoins (L & GRP) | 52 |
| Jenny Lind at Gilfach Ddu (Ian Allan Ltd) | 69 |
| Amalthaea on workmen's train (courtesy Caernarvonshire Record Office) | 69 |
| Hardy petrol locomotive at Gilfach Ddu (courtesy CRO) | 70 |
| Padarn Railway platelayers' bogie (K. Turner) | 70 |
| Assheton-Smith's private saloon coach (L & GRP) | 70 |
| Velocipedes as Gilfach Ddu (courtesy CRO) | 87 |
| Dinorwic Quarry incline (L & GRP) | 87 |
| Gilfach Ddu loading bay (courtesy CRO) | 88 |
| Dinorwic waggon turntable (K. Turner) | 88 |
| Port Penrhyn - *Blanche* and *Winifred* (L & GRP) | 105 |
| Port Penrhyn - standard gauge/narrow gauge crossing (L & GRP) | 105 |
| Port Dinorwic incline (courtesy CRO) | 106 |
| No 1 at Port Dinorwic (L & GRP) | 106 |
| Port Dinorwic (L & GRP) | 106 |
| Penrhyn Railway - *Blanche* on workmen's train (L & GRP) | 123 |

| | |
|---|---:|
| Penrhyn Railway - halfway passing loop *(L & GRP)* | 123 |
| Penrhyn Railway - Coed y Parc yard *(L & GRP)* | 124 |
| Penrhyn Railway - Port engine shed *(K. Turner)* | 124 |
| Penrhyn Quarry - *Jubilee 1897* *(L & GRP)* | 141 |
| Penrhyn Quarry - *Lilla* *(L & GRP)* | 141 |
| Penrhyn Quarry - *Eigiau* *(L & GRP)* | 142 |
| Penrhyn Quarry - *Stanhope* *(L & GRP)* | 142 |
| *Dolbadarn* on the Llanberis Lake Railway *(K. Turner)* | 159 |
| Penscoins 1973 *(K Turner)* | 159 |
| Penllyn level crossing *(K. Turner)* | 160 |
| Pontrhythallt carriage shed *(B. J. Williams)* | 160 |
| Penscoins engine shed *(K. Turner)* | 160 |

IN THE TEXT

| | |
|---|---:|
| General map: railways and tramroads | 12 |
| Diagram: stub points | 36 |
| In the quarry | 39 |
| Map: Penrhyn Railway and Tramroad | 50 |
| Plan: Port Penrhyn | 55 |
| Diagram: port crossing | 57 |
| Waiting at Penscoins | 64 |
| Plan: Gilfach Ddu | 73 |
| Map: Padarn Railway and Tramroad | 75 |
| On the Padarn | 98 |
| On the Penrhyn | 100 |
| Baldwin | 117 |
| Padarn Railway notice re velocipedes *(courtesy CRO)* | 122 |
| Padarn Railway workmen's ticket *(courtesy CRO)* | 126 |
| Padarn Railway notice re workmen's train *(courtesy CRO)* | 126 |
| Instructions to Padarn Railway flagmen *(courtesy CRO)* | 130 |
| *Fire Queen* | 136 |
| Padarn Railway velocipede permit *(courtesy CRO)* | 144 |
| De Winton | 158 |

*Slates here, Slates there,*
  *Slates everywhere,*
*Slates that are large, Slates that are small,*
  *Slates that are short, Slates that are tall,*
*Slates fit for Mangers in the stable,*
  *Slate for the massive Billiard table,*
*Slates for the roofs, Slates for the walls,*
  *Slates for the Schools, Slates for the Halls,*
*Slates that are blue, Slates that are green,*
  *Of varied hues they may be seen,*
*Slates chipped and waste, and thrown to mingle*
  *On the Sea shore among the shingle,*
*Slates line the Wharves where splash the waves,*
  *And in the Churchyard mark the graves.*
            *(—anonymous visitor to Dinorwic Quarry)*

## *Acknowledgements*

I offer grateful thanks to my husband Keith who provided encouragement when it was needed, and understanding at all times. In addition he willingly undertook a considerable share of the donkey-work; proof reading, typing of the manuscript and the like.

I would also like to thank Mr B. J. Williams for his invaluable help in both the fieldwork and the fine drawing of the maps and diagrams. I am also indebted to Tony Coultiss and Peter E. Baughan for many important points of information that otherwise might have passed unrecorded.

Acknowledgements are due to the Archivist and staff of the Caernarvon Record Office for putting up with my many requests; to the Librarian and staff of the University College Library, University of North Wales, Bangor, for similar assistance; and to Hunslet (Holdings) Ltd for kindly allowing me access to official records.

Lastly, I offer my appreciation to all those credited at the beginning of this book for supplying the many photographs and to everyone else who helped in every small way to make it all possible.

CHAPTER I

## The Formative Years

BACKGROUND TO THE SLATE INDUSTRY

Slate has been the mainstay of the North Wales building industry since earliest times. The rise in the population of Wales from 0.2 million in 1500 to 0.4 million in 1700, and similarly throughout Britain as a whole; the coming of the Industrial Revolution and increased conurbation brought a need for a good, cheap roofing material. Slate was ideal—hence a sudden boom in its production.

The Romans used local slate for flooring, as can be seen at Segontium and Caer Llugary in north-west Wales; Edward I used it on Caernarvon and Conway Castles and in 1399 a Frenchman on tour recorded that at Conway there was 'much slate on the houses'. The first known quarries were in the Nantlle Vale and in the Ogwen and Conway valleys and by 1583 slate had become Wales' principal export to Ireland. In 1587 110,000 slates were shipped from Beaumaris and Caernarvon.

The main slate beds in North Wales head from north-east to south-west through Snowdonia from Conway nearly to Pwllheli. Geologically the rocks belong to the Cambrian era and where they outcropped on the surface became quarrying centres. The rock is composed of several beds or veins of workable slate with sandy beds between them. Most of the slates are reddish-purple or blue in colour although some of the upper veins are of a greenish hue. The slates of different

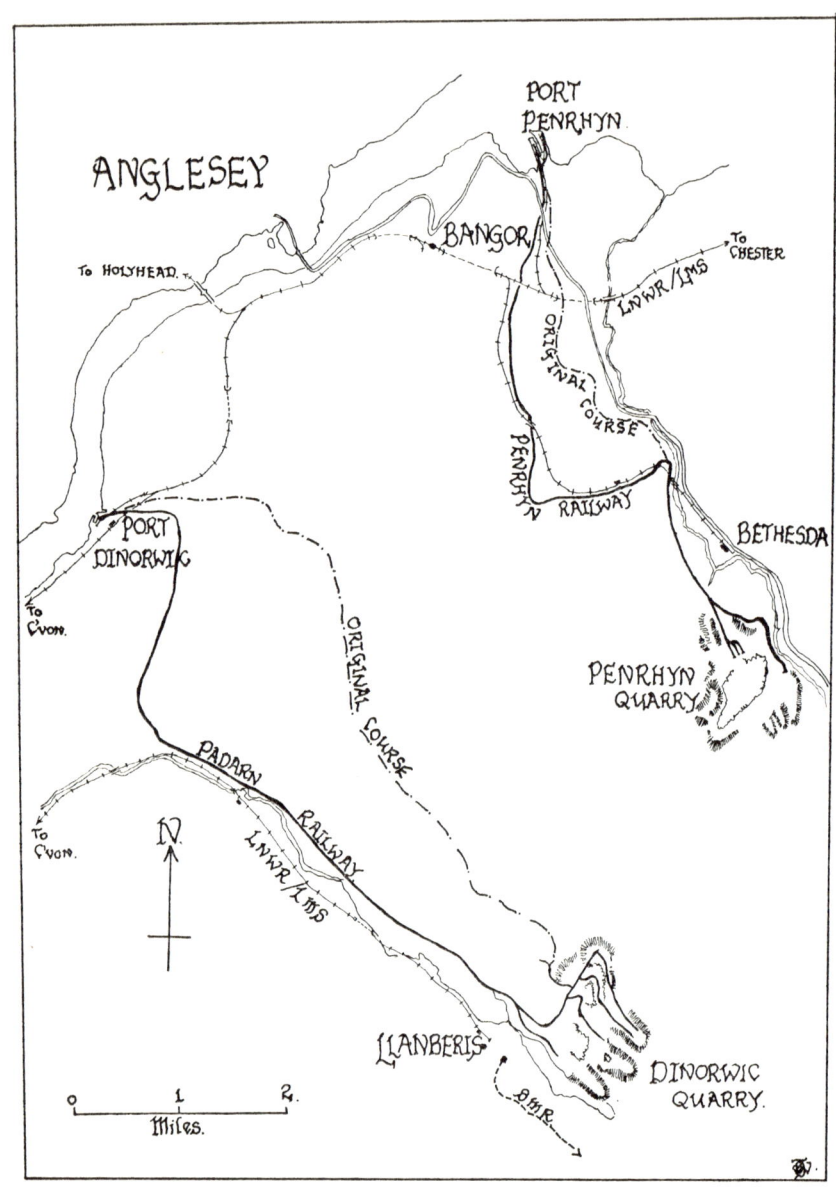

General map showing all railways and original tramroads

## THE FORMATIVE YEARS

veins and those from different parts of the same vein differ in colour and durability. They also differ in the ease with which they can be hewn out of the rock. The names of those slates found in the Dinorwic Quarry illustrate this: green vein, goch galed (hard red), glas galed (hard spotted blue), glas rhywiog (royal blue), goch grychlyd (wrinkled red), hen las (old blue) and the glyn rhonwg vein.

The three main centres of production were always clearly defined and consisted of the areas each side of Elidir Fawr and in the Nantlle Vale. The first two of these, on either side of the 3030ft mountain of Elidir Fawr, were to become the sites of the two most important slate quarries in North Wales, the Penrhyn and the Dinorwic.

### THE PENRHYN ESTATE

Penrhyn Castle and park lay between the rivers Ogwen and Cegin, overlooking the sea to the east of Bangor, whilst the estate stretched southwards from the Menai Straits to Snowdonia, including the northern face of Elidir Fawr. The castle had originally been the site of a Welsh Royal Palace in the eighth century. As early as the fifteenth century slates were being produced on the estate and poems were composed asking for slates from Bangor, thus illustrating that there was a market for them. The first known example was that some time between 1480 and 1502 Guto'r Glyn a noted Welsh bard composed, on behalf of his patron Sir Griffith ap Einion, a cowydd addressed to Dr Richard Kyffin, Dean of Bangor, asking for a cargo of slates to be sent from Aberogwen to Rhuddlan. Towards the end of the sixteenth century a considerable quantity of slates was being exported from here to Ireland.

The slate beds on the Penrhyn estate were let to 'sets' or bands, usually families, of quarrymen who worked their own 'bargains' whilst paying a nominal rent—one item in an estate rent book of 1582 reads 13s 4d 'for the western of the quarries'. The slates were sold to local farmers and used on the neighbouring churches. (Slates from the Penrhyn beds were used on the roof of St Asaph Cathedral in Denbighshire during the reign of Charles I. Some two hundred and fifty years later it was stripped owing to the failure of the timbers and the slates found to be so perfect they were re-used.) For export the slates were transported in horse-borne panniers to the mouth of the Ogwen, Cegin or the Hirael quay in Bangor.

In 1622 the estate became the property of Lord Keeper Williams and was then passed from him to his nephew, Sir Robert Williams. After his death the estate became the joint property of the Warburtons of Cheshire and the Yonges of Devon. The boundaries of the estate and the extent of the owners' rights fell into confusion—even utter chaos. Absent owners knew little if anything of what was happening to their property; estate managers were lax and inefficient and the estate as a whole was neglected. From 1719 to 1736 a Mr Doulben was the agent but in the latter year a 'new broom' was appointed in the figure of John Paynter. In the first flush of enthusiasm he made a few improvements and began a protracted dispute with the Crown over a question of land ownership. Paynter aimed to lease the common land at Cilgwyn in the Nantlle Vale and so cut out competition from the slates produced there as the Cilgwyn slates were far more marketable, being larger, lighter and fetching a lower price than the Penrhyn slates; there was a serious danger of the Penrhyn slates being driven off the market. The plan failed for the Crown claimed the common land and indeed Paynter himself failed as a competent agent—for seven years he omitted to keep any accounts. During this time production fell rapidly and skilled quarrymen left their workings and turned their hands to other things.

In 1736 roughly 2000 tons of slate were produced and the profit to the estate from this was less than £100. Two years later Penrhyn slates were selling for 9s 8d a mille; 2s 8d of this went as royalty to the estate but production remained static. (A mille, nominally one thousand slates, was actually 1200 in number.) In 1746 the new agent, Hughes, reduced prices and royalties in the hope of recapturing custom. He allowed prices to fall by 50% in the hope that Penrhyn could

# THE FORMATIVE YEARS 15

regain its footing and its market. Slates were now only 4s 10d a mille and the royalty had fallen to 1s 4d and later as low as 10d. Whatever steps were taken output repeatedly fell until in 1746 it was barely 482 milles whereas it had been 1852 milles eight years previous. When Lewis Morris published his survey of Welsh ports in 1748 he credited Caernarvon with sales of 4 million slates a year but did not consider Bangor slates worth mentioning. Twenty years later a traveller visiting Bangor would have been unaware of any sea-going traffic other than small fishing vessels, so slight was the exportation of slate.

## BIRTH OF THE PENRHYN QUARRY

In the latter quarter of the eighteenth century, when so much expansion and improvement was carried out in the slate industry, Richard Pennant, son of John Pennant, was lord of the manor at Penrhyn. The Pennant family wealth was founded on a rich sugar plantation in Jamaica; in 1765, at the age of twenty-eight, Richard Pennant had married the heiress of the Warburtons of Cheshire, who had inherited half of the Penrhyn estate. Twenty years later he purchased the other half from the Yonges of Devon. The estate was comparable with its neighbour the Vaynol estate in that both were rich farming properties bringing in large rents. In 1767 Samuel Wright was appointed agent to the Penrhyn estate and on 1 September 1768 fifty-four leases were signed by General Warburton and John Pennant for the slate-workings, letting them to sundry persons at various rents, usually for a period of twenty-one years. A covenant of £1 a year extra was also made in lieu of royalties from the slate. The slate reeve continued to keep accounts and market the slate but inefficiency and negligence on the part of the quarrymen led to chaos, especially as the work was done in a haphazard fashion with no regard for the future development of the workings by clearing away waste rock, planning new excavations and so on.

In 1782, a few years before they were due to expire, Richard Pennant bought the leases out at a cost of £160. He kept the men on as hired labourers and ran the workings himself. He also tried to safeguard a monopoly of quarrying in the district by taking out leases on the neighbouring crown wastes and common land but this policy, naturally, led to many complaints and eventually to a parliamentary inquiry. At this time output was smaller than that of 1738 though remedial action was well under way. When it came to the Pennants the whole Penrhyn estate provided no more than four carts but within ten years paths from the quarry to the coast had been made into negotiable roads with just over 100 carts in regular use upon them. In the 1780s Richard Pennant's slate reeve was William Williams, who had previously worked as a weaver in Anglesey before being apprenticed to a lawyer. He had showed aptitude and great capability and had become a land surveyor on various estates. At Penrhyn he kept accurate and systematic accounts of all workings and dealings—something rarely done before. He was pensioned-off in 1802 at the age of 64 and spent his remaining 15 years in writing. The estate agent at the same time was Benjamin Wyatt, the architect's brother and a good architect himself. He designed houses for the tenants and in 1790 planned the development of Abercegin.

In 1780 the Penrhyn output was 1800 tons. Shipping was a major problem, for vessels preferred to trade with Caernarvon (and hence other quarries) where there were proper port facilities. In 1790, however, Pennant took a lease from Bishop Warren of Bangor for the foreshore at Pen y Bryn and built Port Penrhyn at the mouth of the Afon Cegin, one mile further west from Aberogwen. When the port was being built slates were found buried deep in the mud, giving cause for speculation that there had already existed, at an unknown date, an early export trade from there. In 1792 over 12,000 tons were exported from there whilst in the following year 6645 tons were being exported coastwise, plus 4356 tons to Ireland, making an overall total of 11,001 tons. The North Wales total of slate exports for the year was 23,931 tons. In 1783 (after being MP for Liverpool for some years) Pennant had been made an Irish peer with the right to sit in the House of Commons.

## THE FORMATIVE YEARS

Before the Napoleonic Wars output at Penrhyn had risen to 15,000 tons a year with 4-500 men working in the quarry. Pennant had begun to build his model village of Llandegai for his growing workforce, where, in the words of Thomas Pennant, traveller (and distant relation of Richard), 'no corrupting alehouse' was permitted. The war brought a temporary setback and the project was interrupted for a time. The village was centred round the church of St Tegai, a divine of the fifth century, which parish stretched from the coast to the mountains of Snowdonia. By 1795 the slate trade was feeling the effect of the war and of the tax imposed on coast-bound slate (see later). Output fell to 8000 tons a year and trade declined so much that Pennant was forced to discharge men, though he tried to find them alternative work on his estate so that he could fall back on skilled workers when trade revived. At this time great improvements to the estate were undertaken, notably on the roads, using the redundant quarrymen as his labour force. By 1798 only 120 men were employed at the quarry but slate traffic was significantly increased by a new road from the quarry to the port. It extended nine miles further back inland to Capel Curig and there were 120 broad-wheeled carts being used on it. The road ran entirely on the Penrhyn estate and was to become an important link in Telford's Shrewsbury-Holyhead mail road opened in 1818. In 1788 the cost of slate transport had been 5s 3d per ton, two-thirds of the cost of the slate, but eight years later the cost had dropped to 4s per ton. By 1800 Pennant was employing 140 waggons, 140 men and 400 horses on his new road. During this period the Penrhyn and Dinorwic Quarries were constantly vying with each other, each benefiting from the example set by its neighbour, until finally they came together to deal with strikes, lock-outs and the standardisation of price lists.

### THE VAYNOL ESTATE

The Dinorwic Quarry lay in the parish of Llanddeiniolen (extending from the Menai Straits west of Bangor to the eastern shore of Llyn Padarn and the north-western slopes of

Elidir Fawr) three miles south-west of the Penrhyn Quarry on the other side of the mountain. It was part of the old Crown Manor of Dinorwic which William III had alienated. It was then subject to a nominal rent and other reservations and under these conditions was let to a Hampshire gentleman named John Smith, who served as commissioner of the Salt Office, Thomas Assheton-Smith later succeeding to the estate. Assheton-Smith was the son of Thomas Assheton of Ashley, Cheshire. He added Smith to his name on inheriting the old crown manor (then known as the Vaynol, or Vaenol, estate) and the Tedworth, Hants, estate from his uncle William Smith. He was born in 1752 and from 1774 to 1780 was MP for the county. He became High Sheriff for Caernarvonshire in 1783.

### THE RISE OF THE DINORWIC QUARRY

At the time of Assheton-Smith's inheritance quarrymen were allowed to 'dig' for slates on the Vaynol estate in return for a small consideration to the owner. Over the years operations expanded, innovations were introduced and the loads were sent to Caernarvon or Y Felinheli (the site of a small creek on the Menai Straits) for shipment. By 1787 high profits in the slate industry and the example set by Richard Pennant induced the lord of the manor to work his own slates; Assheton-Smith let the largest of the quarries, the Dinorwic Quarry (by the village of the same name), on a twenty-one year lease to the solicitor of his estate, a lawyer from Caernarvon and a third partner. At first there were only thirty men working for them—those willing to work under new management which held itself responsible for marketing and transporting the slates.

In its beginning the Dinorwic Slate Co (as it was entitled) was not a wealthy concern and times were difficult. There was only one serious incident, though, and that was when within barely six months of its formation the company was forced to pay out over £70 'on purpose to keep the men quiet and prevent them going to the common to open and work quarries for themselves and encroach on Mr Smith's

## THE FORMATIVE YEARS

right thereto'. (Pritchard 1944.) Bailiffs were paid to eject men from their illicit quarries and there were often disturbances amongst the unruly workmen. In the September of 1788 William Bridge, the acting manager, informed his partners that unless the existing balance of £120 for the wages was paid he would be forced to flee the district because of hostilities from the quarrymen. (In fact records show that as late as 1809 'vagabond quarrymen' had taken over the small quarries on the outskirts of the Dinorwic enterprises.)

There was a great deal of mobility between the various quarry works. It is recorded that in February 1789 five Dinorwic men left their works for the Penrhyn Quarry, whilst there were five new workmen from Penrhyn and Cefn Ddu at Dinorwic. Some even branched out alone—one example shows that two men left Dinorwic and started their own quarries on Cefn Ddu common. Old quarrymen were used to independence and for a time some were able to keep hold of their claims or find new ones.

Times improved and within a year profits doubled, then trebled, and by 1791 exports from the Dinorwic Quarry through Caernarvon had reached 2½ million slates a year. This was more than half the port's total trade in slates. Assheton-Smith reaped handsome profits from the quarry (and derived an income of above £25,000 per annum from his landed estates). At this date better roads were built out of the mountains from the quarry to Y Felinheli and the quay here was enlarged in 1793, again following Pennant's example. By now two-thirds of the output from the Penrhyn and Dinorwic works was shipped coastwise to new markets created by new conurbations, new factories and an ever-increasing population. The joint output of the North Wales quarries in 1793 topped 26,000 tons though the quarries now suffered one serious drawback: slates despatched coastwise were subject to duty (while those to Ireland were exempt). Those sent to England carried a duty of 34s a ton on average. This duty was William Pitt's way of giving protection to the English tile makers.

Slates and stone carried by coasting navigation from any

port of Great Britain are subject to a duty of twenty per cent on the value, payable at the port of delivery. Thus it operates both on the material and the carriage. The duty which amounts, on an average to one-third the first cost of the article, with the price of freight, has tended greatly to throw a damp on the trade, and, were it not for the frequent evasions, would be still more injurious.

(Evans 1810)

Slates of a general size were charged for tax and freightage by number and those of larger dimensions by the ton.

## THE DINORWIC QUARRY CO

In 1806 Assheton-Smith promoted an Act of Parliament, passed in 1808, to enclose the parish of Llanddeiniolen. Under this Act the lord's right to take over all existing excavations and machinery was reserved. Quarrymen who had built cottages or opened little quarries on the common land found their livelihood threatened. When Assheton-Smith's lease to the Dinorwic Slate Co ran out in 1809 a new partnership was formed of the owner, who was now fully aware of the quarry's potentialities, his solicitor and a third partner, William Turner, a Lancashire prospector and later general manager. In August of the same year the claims of those displaced cottagers were examined but within a month, before any decision could be reached, some impatient cottagers met on the common in Llanddeiniolen and continued to act riotously even after the Riot Act had been read. Several violent assaults were committed. Five guineas was offered as a reward for anyone contributing information leading to the arrest of the ringleaders, who included William Evan Shon Foulk, Foulk Evan Shon Foulk, Ellis Evan Shon Foulk, all quarrymen, Richard Jones, Margaret Owen and Margaret Hughes. By the end of September all but three were in prison at Caernarvon but were soon released under the amnesty by which the Jubilee of George III was celebrated. The cottagers had gained nothing. Strengthened by the ruthless enforcement of the Llandeiniolen Enclosure Act against any further opposition from individuals,

## THE FORMATIVE YEARS

Assheton-Smith went ahead to build an inclined plane from the quarry face down to Llyn Padarn (thus enabling the slate to travel part of the way to the port by water).

The table below shows the value of the slates sold from Dinorwic, the total cost of production and the percentage rate of profit from 1813 to 1819. Included in the gross profit is the royalty paid to Assheton-Smith who held a half-share in the Dinorwic Quarry Co. (When he took over the ownership of the company completely in 1820 royalty payments ceased but a one-eighth share of the gross profits went to the general manager William Turner.)

| Year | Selling price: £ | Cost of production: £ | Gross profit: £ | Rate of profit: % |
| --- | --- | --- | --- | --- |
| 1813 | 15,518 | 10,384 | 5,133 | 49 |
| 1814 | 14,217 | 10,212 | 4,005 | 39 |
| 1815 | 17,384 | 9,917 | 7,466 | 75 |
| 1816 | 14,051 | 10,261 | 3,788 | 37 |
| 1817 | 19,617 | 10,780 | 8,837 | 82 |
| 1818 | 23,888 | 13,415 | 10,473 | 78 |
| 1819 | 23,451 | 13,907 | 9,544 | 69 |

Right from its beginnings the quarry was worked on a large scale in comparison with most other slate quarries. The main drawback was rising costs—for every ton of slate produced an average of 20 tons of rubbish had to be removed. As the years passed the waste had to be carried further and further away and became an ever-increasing problem. During boom periods the quarry was hindered by the very volume of its trade—work was hampered by the sheer quantity of waste rock that had to be removed. This, naturally, affected efficiency and the management had difficulty meeting the demands of loyal customers who demanded priority in shipment.

Prior to the Napoleonic Wars Welsh slate was shipped to Ireland and coastwise to Liverpool but the tax imposed in 1793 caused the Welsh quarries to open up a foreign market with Flanders, Hamburg and some Danish ports. The figures below give an estimated quantity and proportion of slate sent coastwise and to Ireland in 1793:

|  | Coastwise tons | % of total | To Ireland tons | % of total | Total tons |
|---|---|---|---|---|---|
| Dinorwic Quarry: | 1929 | 73 | 723 | 27 | 2652 |
| North Wales : | 12,564 | 53 | 11,367 | 47 | 23,931 |

The Penrhyn and Dinorwic Quarries were the largest in North Wales at this time, together producing no less than 57% of the total output. 63% of their combined production was shipped coastwise to new markets which had grown up as a direct result of the wave of industrial activity sweeping the country. 1794 brought a slump in domestic demand and output fell but this was temporary. From 1796 to 1802 the slate industry was working at less than half its productive capacity but by 1803 trade had revived and the industry remained fairly prosperous until 1814. At this date the net receipts of the Dinorwic Quarry Co began to fall—in 1816 a small loss was actually noted, owing partly to the expense of purchasing a slate sawing machine at a cost of £550. In the same year further rope-worked inclines and the first tramroads were introduced to make movement and transportation inside the quarry easier, although the old-fashioned wheelbarrows continued to be used in the Dinorwic Quarry for a further fifteen years until 1831.

In 1817 Dawkins Pennant took over the Penrhyn estate (see chapter 3) and he and Assheton-Smith astutely avoided a price war by collaborating in the fixing of prices, thus maintaining, it was hoped, the usual high rate of profit. The Ffestiniog Slate Co co-operated in this venture, mainly because two of the Dinorwic partners held shares in that concern also! In that year, however, buiding revived and the slate industry as a whole experienced a short-lived boom up to 1818 when it reached a new record, only to fall again slightly in 1820 (when Assheton-Smith began to run the quarry alone), this time for a period of fifteen years. When he took over the sole direction of the quarry not only did Assheton-Smith have 8-10 vessels at any one time loading at his enlarged port, removing between them an average of 50 tons a day, but also a labour force of over 200 men.

## THE FORMATIVE YEARS

The quarry continued to thrive and develop. The quarrymen showed skill in their work, machinery was widely employed and expansion of the excavations and radical improvements in their working were carried out. During the whole of this period there was also tremendous agitation for the repeal of the government's slate duty. This finally came to a head when the Welsh industry seemed to be in serious danger of losing its Lancashire market and there were numerous meetings in North Wales and petitions filed. Agitation was successful and culminated in the disappearance of the duty in 1831, thus enabling the industry to forge rapidly ahead.

### EARLY MEANS OF TRANSPORT

Before the introduction of tramroads the carriage of slates from the quarry was somewhat primitive. The original method was by carrying the slates in panniers on pack horses, as had been practised at Penrhyn. Each pannier load was 64 slates. This method was tedious, awkward and dangerous and proved even more inadequate as the industry itself increased in prosperity. Carriage by carts superseded this but again proved almost as slow. The carts each carried about one ton of slates in winter and two tons in summer, a reflection on the different road conditions at the different times of the year. (The Penrhyn carts were reported as holding up to $2\frac{1}{2}$ tons—perhaps indicative of the better roads.) The cart was drawn down the bridle path by one horse in front with another hooked behind as a brake. A later improvement at Dinorwic substituted a loaded sledge at the back of the cart. A contemporary writer suggested, mindful of Pennant's tramroad experiment, that a better idea 'would be an inclined plane, with a proper apparatus attached' (Evans 1810). The cost of carriage rose drastically during boom periods, each company competing to gain the service of the slate carriers by offering increased rates and better conditions in order to obtain a monopoly of traffic. These inducements included the paying of all bills at the turnpikes and not deducting the customary contributions for repairing the roads from the carriers' earnings.

This simple method of cart transport was both unreliable and expensive and by the end of the eighteenth century the cost of conveying Dinorwic slates from quarry to port was greater than the overall cost of production. In 1788 it cost more to bring a ton of slates from the Dinorwic Quarry to Y Felinheli than it did to ship the load from this port to Liverpool.

Transport at the quarry face itself was no more modern but as the excavations spread man-operated winches were introduced to raise the slate blocks and rubbish to the edge of the quarry where buckets of useless rock were emptied into wheelbarrows to be dumped wherever convenient at the time. Nevertheless it was often necessary for the loads to be carried on the quarrymen's shoulders—the men wearing heavy leather jerkins as protection—to a clear space. It seems strange that such tiring work was carried out when tramroads were already in use at a neighbouring copper mine (Evans 1810). All slate rubbish was put as near the outer rim of the pits as possible. This was so as to reduce labour costs but this inefficient method of working hindered any development and resulted in rising production costs. Considerable amounts of dead work had to be done, rubbish and top soil cleared and waste rock carried even further away again: unremunerative work taking up valuable time. As no slates were produced no money was earned for the owners.

In 1798 the manager of the Penrhyn Quarry, James Greenfield (Wyatt's brother-in-law), thought of the idea (which was to prove invaluable for the revival of trade) of working the quarry in regular galleries along which were laid primitive narrow gauge tramroads. These galleries or terraces were to save large quantities of good slate rock, rock that would formerly have been shattered when it fell from the rockface to the earth many feet below. The idea was adopted at Dinorwic in 1799 and by 1830 five terraces had been carved out there. Each followed the contours of the land with a slight decline running from the middle of the terrace outwards in both directions, thus enabling the loaded trucks to run easily along the quarry tramroads introduced in 1816. This reduced the cost of moving slate blocks to the dressing sheds in one direction and rubbish to the margin of the quarry in the other. Rope-worked inclines connected the various terrace levels. Greenfield took great care to establish the extent of the slate strata so that rubbish was not dumped on them. New rubbish was tipped on to other rock beds at Penrhyn or else into Llyn Peris at Dinorwic, although there still remained some former waste material along the slate beds themselves. The valueless outcrops were left standing though this impeded the working of the slate beds on regular lines.

CHAPTER 2

# The Quarries

### THE SLATE

Dinorwic slate was 'unsurpassed for its excellent quality' (*North Wales Slate Quarries* 1920). The produce of the Penrhyn Quarry was no less famous; the slate the two quarries produced was the hardest and the most imperishable available, suitable for all climates and absolutely watertight. It was produced in many varied hues and colours ranging from blue through red and grey to sea-green in the upper veins; it was divided into various qualities, all durable, such as (at Dinorwic) Best and Second Old Quarry, Best and Second New Quarry, Best and Second Green and Wrinkled, Best and Second Mottled, etc. In the volume quoted above, published by the Midland Bank Chambers, Caernarvon, the following is recounted:

> Quite recently a Blackburn slater stripped the roof from a house which was known to have stood unaltered for a hundred years. Dinorwic or Velinheli slates had been used, and he found that they were absolutely as good as new.

In fact the tale continued to relate how the same slates were used for roofing another house. The *Times* of 9 September 1908 had this to say on the subject:

> To question slaters and builders, with a lifetime's experience in their trade behind them, as to the durability or life of a Dinorwic slate is to be told that no limit can be placed on its wearing qualities. Where Dinorwic (Velinheli) slates

are used, the nails which affix them to the roof timbers give way and corrode, while the slates are unaffected. Though the nails are gone, the Dinorwic slates remain as sound and weatherproof as the day they were cut out of the Dinorwic quarry forty, sixty or a hundred years ago.

Slate is impenetrable to the corrosive action of atmospheric acids: Messrs Pilkington Bros of St Helens, one of the largest glass manufacturers in the world, found it necessary to roof their works with Dinorwic slates as nothing else would withstand the gases generated by glass making and the many chemical factories in that town. For similar reasons the Mersey Docks & Harbour Board always stipulated that Dinorwic slates should be used on their sheds and warehouses. The *Times* article continued to illustrate the superiority of the product by stating that the buildings in Clerkenwell of the Holborn Board of Guardians were roofed with foreign slates in 1898 but after only seven or eight years the slates had become so worn that repairs were more or less hopeless; the roof was stripped entirely and re-covered with Dinorwic slates.

Similar tales could be recounted concerning the use of Penrhyn slate—it did, after all, come from the same beds that were quarried at Dinorwic. Suffice to say that in the post-World War I building boom, many owners of newly-built houses were forced to have their roofs stripped and reslated because imported European slates had become porous after less than a dozen years of service.

### SIZES AND PRICES

The small, thick slates of the days prior to standardisation used to sell in the seventeenth and eighteenth century at 5s or 6s a mille. (A mille, nominally a thousand slates, was actually 1200 in quantity.) In May 1788 the Dinorwic Slate Co had nine bargains employing 42 men in all. Five out of the nine received the standard list prices for the slate produced; in the remaining four bargains the list prices paid were slightly above or below the standard rate. This was because it was decided that prices should be varied according to the amount of productivity and the accessibility of the slate. During July 1788 all the bargains were negotiable: the maximum price allowed for making a mille of Duchesses (see below) was 16s 3d and the minimum 3s 6d. At the same time the crews of men in the quarry were receiving not only these varying list prices but also a sum of 1½-3gns for removing rubbish and topsoil.

Classified slates from the more modern-minded quarries in North Wales (such as Penrhyn and Dinorwic) varied in price at the end of the eighteenth century from £3 10s a mille for Duchesses to £1 for Ladies and 11s for Doubles. By 1825 prices had doubled and were to rise yet again the following year. The boom came to a sudden end in late 1826 and a period of turmoil was to follow; law suits, quarrels and divisions were to occur within the industry.

The sizes of the slates sold varied though there had been no accurate classification in the early days. In 1557 for example only two sizes were produced: Singles, 10in x 5in, costing 1s 8d a mille and Doubles, 12in x 6in, costing 2s 8d. Expansion of markets brought the need for a greater range of products and new sizes were introduced. The smallest were still Singles and these were followed by Doubles, Double Doubles, Double Double Doubles and so on. It was not until 1738 that a serious attempt at classification was undertaken when the joint owner of the Penrhyn estate, Gen Warburton, introduced the following graduations. Singles and Doubles remained unchanged, Double Doubles became Ladies, Double Double Doubles became Countesses, and then Duchesses, Marquises and Queens. In the twentieth century these names were still being used by the quarrymen although in the trade the slates were classified by their width and lengths and were sold by weight.

In 1788 the Dinorwic quarrymen were divided into their customary crews, with 2-12 men in each crew (the usual number being 4). Each crew worked together in a bargain (their section of the quarry). Remuneration of each crew depended on the number of slates produced and on the nature of the bargain and they were paid according to a graduated series of list prices. In 1788 there were five sizes of tally or tale slates produced (so called because they were of standard size and sold by the mille) and two kinds of ton slates which were very large—or very small—and were sold by weight. Some of the prices for these have survived and are listed below.

| Type | Size | List price |
|---|---|---|
| Countesses | Not under 19in × 10in | 14s 6d per mille |
| Ladies | Not under 15in × 8in | 8s 0d per mille |
| Doubles | Not under 12in × 6in | 4s 0d per mille |
| Ton slates | All sizes | 7s 6d per ton |

New price lists were issued each January; the price of slate in North Wales was at most times decided by the Penrhyn and Dinorwic Quarries which, being the largest concerns, consulted each other and drew up similar price lists.

By 1830 there were ten sizes of tally slates and three kinds of ton slates; 20 years later this had risen to eleven sizes of tally slates and six kinds of ton slates. In the early 1860s North Wales slates were divided into three grades: best, seconds and thirds; in 1870 a fourth grade was introduced. (In the Dinorwic Quarry however only two qualities of slates were distinguished, firsts and seconds, but these were each subdivided into four classes depending upon which vein they had originated from: Old Quarry; New Quarry; Red; and Green and Wrinkled.) All through the 1870s new sizes were continually being introduced and by 1880 there were no less than 32 sizes of tally slates and six kinds of ton slates. Despite this all the different sizes were rigidly standardised. The producers and slate merchants, unlike the quarrymen, now thought in terms of length and breadth. The large number of sizes was so as not to waste valuable slate: standard lengths were produced in a variety of widths, eg 18in long slates could be 9in, 10in or 12in wide. The First quality slates were $\frac{1}{5}$in thick and the Seconds about $\frac{1}{4}$in; Thirds were $\frac{1}{3}$in thick. Nonconventional sizes of slates were rarely—if ever—produced.

### WORKING IN THE QUARRIES

In the nineteenth century the quarry workings usually

employed a joiner, a smith, a few miners, so many labourers, rockmen and quarrymen, a clerk and a manager. The Dinorwic workings covered an area of not less than one square mile in 1859; the depth of slate had never been ascertained but was supposed to have been between 1500ft and 2000ft. The rock in the quarry was worked to a depth of 300ft below ground level and anyone standing

> at the door of the Victoria Hotel Llanberis, hears with interest and admiration the incessant echo of the hammers, and watches the busy movements of the workmen [2400 at this time] clinging apparently to the almost perpendicular sides of the cliffs.
>
> (*Thomas Assheton Smith* 1859)

As has been mentioned before, because the Dinorwic Quarry was situated on a mountainside (which allowed room for the tipping of rubbish) it could be worked in galleries similar to those created by James Greenfield at the Penrhyn Quarry. These galleries were terraces cut into the rockface like gigantic steps, from the bottom to the top. The lowest levels were in the form of pits beneath the water level of Llyn Peris but these were consequently more difficult to work and were later flooded. Each terrace, of which there were five in use by 1830 and thirteen by the quarry's closure, had its own rubbish tip at one end. Here rubble was deposited on top of worthless rock away from the working face or was tipped down the mountainside into Llyn Peris. At Penrhyn spoil heaps were built up away from the rockface. The labourers cleared the soil or shale, the rockmen (*creigiwyr*) followed the labourers and removed the bad top rock from the new gallery and the quarrymen (*chwarelwyr*) worked the actual slate bargains. In all, the galleries reached a height of 2000ft above sea level at Dinorwic and 1300 ft at Penrhyn. The height of a gallery working face was 60-75ft. First quality slates were chiefly produced at the highest levels.

The quarrymen worked their bargains (or specified sections of a gallery) in widths of about 18ft. These men were paid an agreed price for the amount of rock hewn, although as the slate was more difficult to work in some sections the price was proportionately increased. Labourers and rockmen were also paid according to the amount of rock removed—payment at Dinorwic and Penrhyn, as in virtually all the North Wales quarries, was by the ton or by the yard and never by the day.

A number of boys of 14 or 15 years of age began their work as future quarrymen by collecting the odds and ends of broken slate, picking out those pieces which might be of some use and wheeling them in small waggons along the gallery tramroads to the huts where they would be trimmed and turned to account. This apprenticeship, according to 1946 figures, lasted six years. Their wages increased annually. The first year (c1946) it would be at a daily rate of 4s 3d; the second 5s 3d; the third 6s 5d; the fourth 8s 9d and then 10s 2d up to a maximum during the sixth and final year of 12s 3d. After the first completed year of his work the apprentice was known as a 'journeyman learner'. He was sometimes subsidised by that group of quarryman contractors to whom he was attached and who paid his wages after the first year. In 1874 the quarrymen earned an average of 5s and ordinary labourers 3s 10d a day.

The slate was first loosened by blasting with gunpowder (or dynamite in very hard beds). Holes were bored into the rock and the explosive inserted. A hooter was sounded every other hour to signal the stoppage of all work as rock falls were imminent. The men retired to their simple but strongly-built stone shelters where they were allowed to enjoy a pipe for ten minutes or so—the only time smoking was permitted. The explosions vibrated and the shattered rock fell, breaking the reigning silence. After the 'peace hooter' the men left their huts to examine the results and would set to work using hammer and chisel, or a crowbar, to pull down the loosened blocks of slate and then break them into pieces of a more manageable size. (In July 1857 220,000 tons of rock were brought down in one such blast in the Wellington area of the Dinorwic Quarry). A convenient network of tramroads existed upon which small waggons were run. Upon these the rough slate slabs were loaded and taken to the inclines where they were let down by wire ropes to the nearest splitting and dressing shed (*gwal*).

The splitting of the slates was comparatively easy. On a small plot of ground 2-3 yards long by 2 yards wide, adjoining the shed (which was often roughly and unskilfully built and generally narrow, damp, dark and low-roofed), the slate slabs were tapped by the labourers as they arrived, as sometimes they were broken or damaged by careless handling in transit and therefore rendered useless. The quarrymen prepared the slabs for splitting. First they were cleaved into roughly slate-sized blocks with wooden mallets, then a block was taken and a broad chisel and a hammer applied to the edge, causing the slates to split off easily and smoothly, one at a time. These were then taken into the dressing shed for the dresser (*brasholltwr*) to dress them. With the rough edges trimmed off the finished slates were ready to be taken by waggon to the inclines and let down the precipitous side of the mountain to the main collection tramroad, ready for dispatch.

### VISITORS

Besides the royal visits covered elsewhere, notable visitors were allowed, in the nineteenth and twentieth centuries, to ride up the Penrhyn and Dinorwic inclines (in carriages constructed especially for that purpose) and thus tour the workings. This would indeed have been an adventure for the average traveller and required a great deal of courage for although every precaution was taken to prevent danger (no accidents are known to have occurred on these occasions), the stoutest heart may well yet have throbbed with apprehension as its owner, in making the ascent, looked down into the void many hundreds of feet below. The descent must have been no less frightening!

The final royal visit to the Dinorwic Quarry came at a time when it was nearing its closure. Princess Margaret and the Earl of Snowdon visited Caernarvonshire on Wednesday 16 and Thursday 17 May 1962. At the end of their stay, on the Thursday, they paid a visit to the quarry. The princess and

Page 33:
(left) *Course of the village Tramway between the Dinorwic Tramroad and the Dinorwic Quarry, 1973;* (below) *foot of the first Deiniolen incline on the Dinorwic Tramroad. In the centre of the picture the course levels, turns left through 90° and descends the second incline, 1973*

Page 34:
(above) *The old and the new. At the top of the Dinas incline on the Penrhyn Tramroad: the railway veers west while the tramroad formerly continued straight down the hillside;* (below) *Penrhyn Tramroad course at Llandegai, looking towards Bethesda, 1973*

THE QUARRIES 35

her husband were conveyed by diesel train in the two yellow carriages used on special occasions (see Chapter 7). The visitors saw the new brick plant, viewed the small private museum and eventually rode up four inclines to a height of 1500ft whence they had a glorious and vast view of the various operations.

### DINORWIC TRAMROADS

As has been mentioned above, each gallery had its own tramroad with branches leading away to the rock face. These branches were of a lighter, simpler construction and easily moved to where they were required. At the rockface the men manhandled the slate blocks or waste rock into waggons which were pushed (or horse-hauled in the early days) to the main gallery tramroad from where they were drawn, originally by horse and later by locomotives, to the incline—or dressing shed if there was one on that level. By 1859 there were 23 miles of tramroads in the quarry.

Steam locomotives were introduced from 1870 onwards in ever increasing numbers. (Details of these are given in Chapter 7.) Eventually there was at least one for each gallery. They had a motley assortment of names, the origins of many of which are now a mystery; some took these enigmatic labels from race horses, eg *Cloister*, *Jerry M* and *Cackler*, all with which Sir Charles Garden Duff Assheton-Smith won the Grand National. There was a small locomotive shed on each gallery, usually adjacent to the incline. These were simply for keeping the engine in when not required and were constructed, as would be expected, from waste pieces of slate.

The maximum gradient along the galleries was 1 in 41, the maximum curvature of the locomotive-worked lines 53ft radius and the maximum permitted speed 20mph. Approximately 40,000 tons of rock were being moved annually by 1963 but by then, of course, the scale of operations had sharply declined and the majority of the galleries—on which diesel locomotives had been introduced in 1935—were either disused or converted to road transport.

c

The rails used were of bullhead section on the 'main lines' and weighed 44lb per yard. They stood in cast iron chairs (ex-Gilfach Ddu works) on wood sleepers 3ft apart. Where hand propulsion was used 3in x ¾in (or occasionally 3in x 1in) mild steel bars were set on edge in notched sleepers—easily movable and very flexible trackwork. The points used where the engines worked were stub points on account of the waggons' double-flanged wheels and were operated in theory

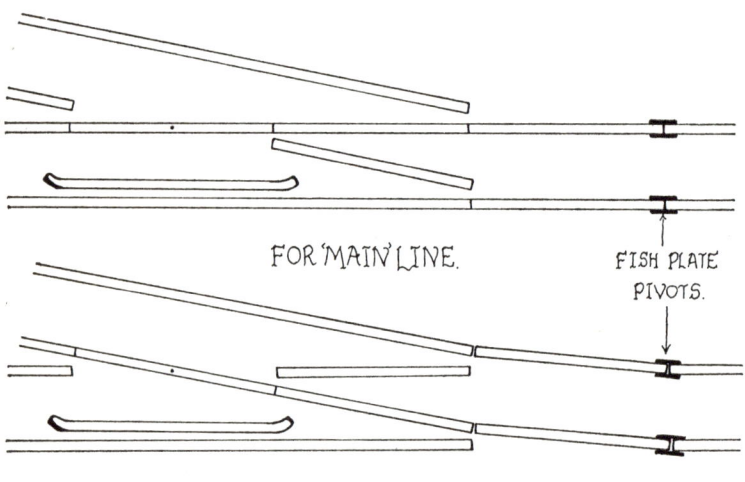

by a hand lever but in practice often by a well-aimed kick! On the branches off the main gallery tramroads to the workface, where the waggons were manhandled, the points became simpler: the moveable sections disappeared and the wheel flanges crossed the junction gaps on steel plates or iron castings. In 1906 the main tramroads amounted to 9 miles 1483yd of track; the '1in road' 3 miles 680yd and the '¾in road' no less than 31 miles 431yd. The total length of the system reached over 50 miles at its greatest extent between the wars; by 1963 there was just 6 miles left; by 1968, ¼ mile.

The inclines were laid on gradients of between 1 in 6 and 1 in 2. The predominant, self-acting sort had a large drum at the top controlled by a band brake. A steel cable wound round the drum with one end attached to loaded trucks at the top and the other to the empty ones at the bottom. It possessed a double track and when the brake was released the loaded trucks ran down by gravity and hauled up the empty ones. The rails used on the inclines were either 3in x 1in bars in notched sleepers or flat-bottom rails in chairs. Each winding house, and thus the incline, was numbered according to its gallery; some galleries were connected with the inclines at various points between top and bottom. This sort of incline had a capacity of three loaded waggons and was worked by two men. The second sort was the tank incline which carried four waggons on a special horizontal platform. On the second track ran another platform carrying a large metal tank. This was filled with water or emptied to make it go up or down in opposition to the weight of the loaded or empty trucks. The 1in steel cables used on the inclines were generally of 30 tons breaking strain.

By 1938 electrically operated ropeways had been introduced. Known as 'Blondin' ropeways and manufactured by Clarke Chapman, these consisted of cables strung between strategic points of the quarry; from them hung vertical pulley ropes for lifting and transporting blocks too large to be handled otherwise.

In 1954 a serious rock fall in the centre of the quarry resulted in a major part of the quarrying being confined to the eastern side of the workings. The fall had cut through all the levels A5A to A7T inclusive; after 1960 it developed further and by 1964 only A9A-C10T and above were left intact.

## PENRHYN TRAMROADS

Basically the workings at the Penrhyn Quarry were on much the same lines as at Dinorwic, with the exception of there being large-scale working of quarry pits below the main (Office) level. The origins of the gallery system have already been dealt with; by the 1870s there were sixteen in use. These were sometimes named after old quarrymen, eg Bonc William

Parry; other names related to the position of the gallery, eg Ceiling being the topmost and Garret the next under Ceiling. Occasionally these galleries, opened from the top of the quarry downwards, were named at opening after visits of members of the royal family, eg Princess Alice sited above Princess Mary. In Welsh the galleries were severally known as *bonciau* (benches). Their names can also indicate the time of opening, eg Crimea (1854-6) or Sebastopol (1854-5). Much can be gleaned from these gallery names!

By 1920 there were 20 galleries in all, each being approximately 60ft high, with its own tramroad as at Dinorwic. By 1946 there were 21 in use, of a combined height of 1200ft and a total length of workface equal to 14 miles, together with 50 miles of tramroad.

The quarry pits were reached first by aerial ropeways and later also by a system of hydraulic lifts from the Office level. Waggons were shunted in the pits by hand until the late 1950s when internal combustion locomotives were introduced. The lifts were abandoned and the rail systems closed when roadways were built into the quarry in the mid 1960s. The ropeways lifted the actual waggons, rather than the slate blocks, but these were later replaced in the main by hydraulic lifts working on much the same principle as the tank inclines at Dinorwic, except that they were vertical and raised the loaded waggons up rather than down. These water balances hoisted rubbish and slate from the quarry pits; an empty truck in one cage descended under the weight of a water-filled tank, raising a second cage with a loaded waggon and an empty tank. The first tank was then emptied and the second filled and the whole process was then ready to be repeated.

The mill and tip levels were the series of levels reached by inclines from the Office level. These were connected direct to the galleries in the mountainside at one end and to the tip heaps at the other. Waggons would also journey to the end of these lines to tip the waste brought up from the quarry pits. All these levels above the Office level were closed during the first three months of 1965 leaving only the pits in production.

There was an extensive system of drainage tunnels in the

quarry connecting with the main 7ft x 6ft adit which discharged into the Ogwen a mile away. Water from levels below this, ie in the pits (and the water used to operate the hydraulic lifts), was pumped into the main adit—as much as 10,000 gallons a minute had to be moved after heavy rain.

Until 1876, when steam locomotives were first introduced, horses were used on the main tramroads—as at Dinorwic—but these were soon superseded and the quarry was exclusively steam operated until 1932, when internal combustion engines began to be used. Even so, in 1964 five steam locomotives were still working. Further details of the quarry locomotives and rolling stock are given in Chapter 5.

Quarry trackwork was more varied than at Dinorwic. The main tramroads were laid with flat-bottom rail spiked to wood sleepers and incorporated stub points similar to those at Dinorwic. The more important of the non-locomotive worked lines were laid with bulb-section rails held in cast iron sills; points were of the fixed variety using cast iron junctions. The most temporary lines utilised round rails with either lift-over 'spoon' points (whereby one set of rails simply physically rested on top of the other) or cast iron junctions with short movable bars to direct the wheels.

CHAPTER 3

# The Penrhyn Railway

### THE PENRHYN TRAMROAD

By the end of the eighteenth century Penrhyn Quarry was thriving, exporting as much as 15,000 tons of slate a year—three or four times as much as that exported by Dinorwic—and a means of transport to the port other than horse-drawn carts was imperative. Demand had outstripped production and the need for efficient and cheaper transport was such that it caused serious problems—problems solved in October 1800 when the construction of the Penrhyn Tramroad was begun. The tramroad was designed by the estate agent Benjamin Wyatt of Lime Grove, near Bangor at the mouth of the Cegin. It was completed in July 1801 and was to make a valuable contribution to narrow gauge railway development by deviating from the normal type of tramroad rails then in use. It is described thus by Wyatt in the *Repertory of Arts and Manufactures* Vol III, second series, 1803:

> The rail hitherto made use of in most railways is a flat one, three feet in length, with a rib on one edge, to give it strength, and to prevent the wheels (which have a flat rim) from running off. Observing that these rails were frequently obstructed by stones and dirt lodging on them; that they were obliged to be fastened to single stones or blocks on account of their not rising sufficiently high above the sills to admit of gravelling the horsepath; that the sharp rib standing up was dangerous for the horses; that the strength

of the rail was applied in the wrong way; and that less surface would create less friction, led me to consider if some better form of rail could not be applied; the oval presented itself as the best adapted to correct all the faults of the flat rail, and I have the satisfaction to say that it has completely answered the purpose in a railway lately executed for Lord Penrhyn, from his Lordship's slate-quarries in Caernarvonshire, to Port Penrhyn (the place of shipping). The wheel made use of on this rail has a concave rim, so contrived in its form, and the wheels so fixed on their axes, as to move with the greatest facility in the sharpest curves that can be required.

The tramroad, commencing opposite Ogwen Bank beside the Afon Ogwen at the western limit of the quarry, ran in a northerly then westerly direction, skirting the quarry, to Coed y Parc. It continued northwards from here, leaving the quarry area, over two minor roads (crossed on the level) to the top of the first incline, Cilgeraint, one mile from its start. It carried on northwards across what is now the B4366 Bethesda-Caernarvon road to the second or Dinas incline, 350ft above sea level, a further mile from the first incline. After passing under a minor road it followed the Ogwen to Halfway Bridge. The tramroad then turned west sharply before bearing north again to Llandegai, 160ft above sea level, where it crossed another minor road. It then followed the Llandegai-Bangor road (A5) before tunnelling under it—the line was now running in the Penrhyn Castle grounds—to the Marchogion incline which took it down to the Afon Cegin which it crossed via a single-arch bridge before reaching Port Penrhyn, $6\frac{1}{4}$ miles from its commencement.

The tramroad was worked with an unknown number of 4-wheeled waggons coupled in trains of 24 to a train, each waggon weighing approximately 3 cwt and having cast iron wheels 12-14in in diameter. These waggons each carried one ton of slate and six loaded trains passed through each stage between inclines in the course of a day, thus giving a theoretical capacity for the line of 144 tons of slate per day. Each train was drawn by two horses; the waggons were probably wooden, low and roughly made, with their wheels loose on loose axles, but they served their purpose and in the long run proved not only more efficient than the carts but far cheaper to operate:

> the saving in power effected was such that . . . *ten* horses were found sufficient to conduct a traffic which had, on a common road, required *four hundred*.
>
> (*Penny Cyclopaedia* Vol XIX 1841)

The three inclines were double and self-acting, the longest extending 220yd, and the loaded waggons were lowered down these three at a time. This action was controlled by means of a winch and brake on the winding drum so that the three full waggons were steadily let down while three empty waggons at the bottom were gradually drawn up. Only a dozen or so men were needed to work the entire line.

One fatal accident is known to have occurred on the Penrhyn Tramroad, near the end of its working life, at about 6.00 pm on Wednesday 7 April 1875. The train involved was probably the last train of the day, returning workers to Bangor; it was also loaded with slates. A slightly inebriated Irish pedlar, Martin Riley, was walking along the road near Halfway Inn, saw the train and decided to take a lift on one of the rear waggons. Unfortunately he fell off almost immediately and the last two or three heavily laden trucks passed over him. The men riding at the front of the train saw the incident and stopped the horses. Riley was taken to Bangor infirmary but died soon after from his injuries.

### PENRHYN QUARRY

> The slates were, for a long time, conveyed to the port by means of carts, at a very heavy expense. But lately an iron tram-road has been completed, which runs entirely from the quarry, and round the quay, an extent of six miles. This is a work nothing but Genius could have contrived and energy executed.

Thus wrote the Rev J. Evans in 1810. As many as 100 tons of

slate a day were conveyed over this new tramroad from the start though traffic often had to cease for a while owing to strong head-winds! With the opening the cost of transport dropped from 4s to under 1s a ton. The tramroad quickly paid for itself against maintenance, accidents, the cost of men and horses and broken slates.

In 1801 a slate saw-mill was set up by the port on the Afon Cegin and from 1803 onwards the Liverpool firm of Messrs Worthington & Co, of which Samuel Holland (renowned for his work in the Ffestiniog region in connection with the slate industry) was a partner, was responsible for the manufacture of mantelpieces, hearth stands, chimney pieces, sepulchre monuments and the like. A factory was also built at the port to cater for the growing demand for school writing slates and blackboards. (Up to this time writing slates had been provided by Swiss manufacturers but now Welsh school slates were coming into their own.) Within twelve months a thriving business had been established at Port Penrhyn and 136,000 slates were exported in that year; 3000ft of timber being used to frame them and 25-30 men employed to carry out the work. Worthington & Co also controlled the shipping and marketing of all the slate produce from the quarry.

A mill was also erected on the Afon Ogwen. This was used to grind quartz and chert for the use of the Staffordshire potteries—an industry in which Worthington & Co had extensive interests. Within a few years the agreement between Pennant and Worthingtons had ended but Mr Worthington continued his work at Port Penrhyn, taking on his own shoulders all responsibility for shipping and selling the slate (presumably for the same 6% commission). Flints were also ground at the Ogwen mill; these were brought over as ballast in the empty Irish slate vessels. Manganese ore was prepared at the mill, for bleaching purposes, and zinc ore was similarly treated for use as an alternative to white lead in pigments and paint.

Pennant built a beautiful lodge at Ogwen Bank, by the quarry, for the use of his family and guests, but his enjoyment of it was short-lived for he died in 1808. He left no children and his wife died soon after him. His sister's grandson, George Hay Dawkins (later Dawkins-Pennant), succeeded to the estate. At this date the quarry was making approximately £7000 per annum profit.

The quarry was heavily hit by the Napoleonic Wars, losing both custom and skilled men. But this slump was only temporary and work revived so that in the post-war years over 300 men were employed at the quarry, rising to a new record of 874 in 1812. These figures are indicative of the expansion and the success of the workings during this period. Dawkins-Pennant erected the chapel of St Anne near the quarry in 1813, at a cost of £2000. The land opposite the quarry in the parish of Llanllechid was owned by yeomen farmers who let or sold plots to the quarrymen. It was here that in 1820 a small group of men from Llandegai built, on a site close to an alehouse (sorely lacking at Llandegai) and a group of quarrymen's cottages, their own chapel, naming it Bethesda. Within the space of ten years the growing village was known by that name and the chapel was later rebuilt and enlarged in 1830 and again in 1840. By 1865 the population was nearing 6000 —more than four times that of 1801.

In 1819 the output of the Penrhyn Quarry (and hence traffic over the tramroad) was 24,418 tons, valued at £58,000 and included 802 crates of writing slates. The protracted dispute with the Crown still continued but some settlement appears to have been reached in 1823, according to a letter of 11 November from Gifford & Copley, attorney and solicitor-general respectively of Lincoln's Inn:

> We are of the opinion that there is no sufficient evidence . . . to establish the rights of the crown to the common in the parish of Llandegai and that the possession and repeated acts of ownership exercised by the Penrhyn family render it, in our judgement, impossible to hope for success in any proceedings to be instituted by the Crown to obtain possession of this property.

Dawkins-Pennant thus won the ownership of the common land.

## THE PENRHYN RAILWAY 45

The early 1820s were boom years for the quarry with 1200 men employed there. In 1825 150 men struck for higher wages but to no avail. The 1826 output topped 45,000 tons for the first time whilst over 500 cargoes were cleared at the port; 1827 saw 47,000 tons surpassed but this was followed rapidly and depressingly by a fall in production (as well as prices) down to 39,000 tons. The strike had brought a new manager to Penrhyn, one who made improvements in transport, blasting techniques and tools. He was able to see the quarry safely through the slump with very little loss into 1830 when 1400 men were at work and 5-600 tons of slate were raised daily. In 1827 Dawkins-Pennant had pulled down the old family mansion and started to build a pseudo-Norman monstrosity (designed by Wyatt) in its place—the present Penrhyn Castle.

Thankfully, for the quarry proprietors of North Wales, the 1793 tax levied on coast-bound slate was lifted in 1831 and by 1839 Penrhyn output had leapt to 73,738 tons, selling for £124,667 and yielding a profit of £62,144. Dawkins-Pennant died in 1841 and was succeeded by his son-in-law Edward Gordon Douglas, born in 1800 and a member of one of the most aristocratic families in Scotland. He became Douglas-Pennant by the queen's warrant and sat in the Commons for Caernarvonshire in the same year. At this date the income of the estate was reputed to be no less than £250,000 per annum.

During the late 1840s the standard gauge reached the district in the form of the Chester & Holyhead Railway (C & HR), opened through to Bangor in 1848. It passed under the Penrhyn Tramroad in a short tunnel south of Llandegai; the tunnel was necessitated by the terrain—though Douglas-Pennant had secured good protection for his tramroad in the C & H incorporating Act of 1844 which stated that the railway company could not interfere during or after construction with any of Douglas-Pennant's quarry tramroads or railways built beside or across its route,

> or either permanently or temporarily, to take, alter, interfere with, or use, or to obstruct or anywise impede the free passage upon or along any of the said present or future Rail-

ways or Tramroads (or any Part thereof) to, from, or in connexion with the said Mines or Quarries or any of them.

(7 & 8 Vic c65 clause 264)

1845 was a 'boom' year for the Penrhyn Quarry with a labour force of nearly 3000 men at work: taking workmen, boatmen and families into consideration there were almost 15,000 people supported by the one quarry alone, with a weekly wage bill totalling £1643 10s.

> This immense sum is expended in this neighbourhood. No wonder then that Bangor and its inhabitants are in such a flourishing condition. Well may their standing toast be "the blue veins of Arfon", which is responded to with heartfelt feeling by every individual in this part of the country.

(Parry 1848)

The following year, 1846, saw Penrhyn's second strike. By 1848 the tramroad was regularly carrying over 50,000 tons of slate each year. By 1859 the Penrhyn estate was the richest in North Wales with an annual net profit from the quarry alone of £100,000. In 1865 there were twenty times as many workers (nearly 6000) as there had been at the beginning of the century; that year saw the quarry's third strike. This time a union was formed but it was only temporary as it could not withstand the pressures put upon it by Dawkins-Pennant who, in the following year, was raised to the British peerage as Lord Penrhyn.

### PERMANENT WAY

(The following details of the Penrhyn Tramroad permanent way have been compounded from a collection of contemporary sources. For further reference see *Bibliography*.)

In 1825 Thomas Tredgold noted that the oval section cast iron rails were 4ft 6in long and that they

> wore the concave rims of the wheels very fast into a hollow, fitting so close to the road as to create much friction, and oblige them to change the wheels often.

THE PENRHYN RAILWAY 47

This problem of wheels binding on the rails gives the reason as to why the rail section was soon altered to a solid U shape to give a flat running surface for flat-rimmed double-flanged wheels. The rails were of the fish-bellied pattern then in vogue and weighed 36lb for each 4ft 6in length. A thicker section at each end slotted into a cast iron chair cast integrally with a cross-sill and second chair. The whole sill unit weighed 14lb.

Two Prussian visitors to the tramroad, von Oeynhausen and von Dechen, stated in 1829 that the rails were only 3ft long and of an elliptical cross section $1\frac{3}{4}$in high and $1\frac{1}{4}$in wide. The chairs in which the rails simply rested (or were occasionally spiked) were 8in long by 6in wide. The cross-sills rested on stone sleepers—presumably a block under either chair since the sills were bow-shaped. Fishplates were not apparently in use and the chairs were the only link between the rail ends.

Both Tredgold and the Prussian engineers gave the gauge as being 24in. This was almost certainly between the rail centres with the oval section rails; when these were changed to give a flat running surface with $1\frac{1}{4}$in wide rails in the same chairs the gauge would have altered to an inside rail measurement of 1ft $10\frac{3}{4}$in. Any argument that the '2ft gauge' used in North Wales is in some way mysteriously related to a precise 60cm gauge (1ft $11\frac{5}{8}$in) is entirely spurious since there were as many, if not more, variations round the 24in mark as there were round the 4ft $8\frac{1}{2}$in in the early days of the standard gauge.

A NEW LINE

The Penrhyn Railway was surveyed and mapped out by Charles Easton Spooner of Festiniog Railway fame during the period 1877-8; his final plans are dated 30 June 1878. The idea of a new route avoiding the use of any inclines between the quarry and the port had only recently been formulated. The management had previously considered it pointless to follow the Padarn's example (see Chapter 4) and construct a wider gauge line and be subsequently met with transhipment problems merely for the sake of using steam locomotives. With the industry booming however the Penrhyn Tramroad was working at its full capacity—indeed it could barely cope with the traffic and expansion became a greater necessity. It had not been until the 1860s that the Festiniog Railway proved that steam traction could be successfully used on a 2ft gauge; the resulting benefits reaped by the Festiniog gave impetus to the Penrhyn management and on 17 July 1875 the *Caernarvon & Denbigh Herald* announced:

> We understand that Lord Penrhyn has decided upon running a locomotive engine on the tramway along which the slates are conveyed from the quarry to the port.

It appears that this scheme was soon dropped as impractical considering the nature of the Penrhyn Tramroad, broken as it was by its inclines, and the idea of a new railway then emerged. This incidentally coincided with a local movement to promote an independent, or GWR or LNWR backed, standard or narrow gauge line between Bethesda and Bangor. Many different routes and ideas were proposed, some though not all meeting with strong opposition from Lord Penrhyn, and nothing came of the plan until the LNWR opened its branch to Bethesda in 1884.

In February 1877 Lord Penrhyn's agent informed the LNWR that he intended to construct a new railway, to the same gauge as the tramroad, between the quarry and Port Penrhyn and this would be worked by steam locomotives. With Spooner engaged to prepare the necessary plans, a contractor for the new line was sought. On 9 March 1878 the *Caernarvon & Denbigh Herald* reported that

> The contract for the construction of a two-feet gauge railway, extending from Port Penrhyn, Bangor, to Tregarth in connection with the Penrhyn Slate Quarries, has been let to Mr Richard Parry, Menai Bridge. The contract will occupy about two years in execution, and will give employment to a large number of men. Mr Algeo, Menai Bridge, is the engineer in charge of the works.

The reference to Tregarth refers to the point where the new

railway was to join the old tramroad. The latter's gauge of 1ft 10¾in was retained and the track laid with flat-bottom rails on wooden sleepers.

Despite the prediction that it would take two years to construct, the railway was completed in less than one. The precise date of its opening is unknown but it was definitely working by February 1879. In fact, references to the proposed Bangor-Bethesda standard gauge line in December 1878 imply that the Penrhyn Railway was already constructed, and presumably actually in operation, by then. To work the slate trains three locomotives were ordered from de Winton & Co of Caernarvon, suppliers of seven quarry locomotives to Penrhyn. Further details of these, and the other Penrhyn Railway locomotives, are given in Chapter 5.

THE ROUTE DESCRIBED

The Penrhyn Railway started at Coed y Parc by the quarry workshops complex and was connected there, by incline, to the internal quarry system and from there to the old tramroad round the edge of the quarry. The line left the quarry area to the east of the tramroad exit, passing under Coed y Parc road and heading north. A few hundred yards further on, high above the roadway on its right, it crossed another minor road which dived beneath it having crossed the tramroad course higher up the hillside on the level. The original line soon dropped down to the level of the railway by means of the Cilgeraint incline which was crossed by the new route; from then on both the old and the new lines occupied roughly the same trackbed. Continually dropping in height, the railway reached the level of its parallel roadway at its only level crossing, Hendurnpike, 1½ miles from the quarry.

The level crossing was a somewhat involved one for whilst in the process of turning slightly across the road beside it, to follow the right-hand lane from the junction at that point, the railway had also to negotiate another minor road which helped to complicate the situation. The result was approximate to a crossroads junction with the railway bisecting it diagonally;

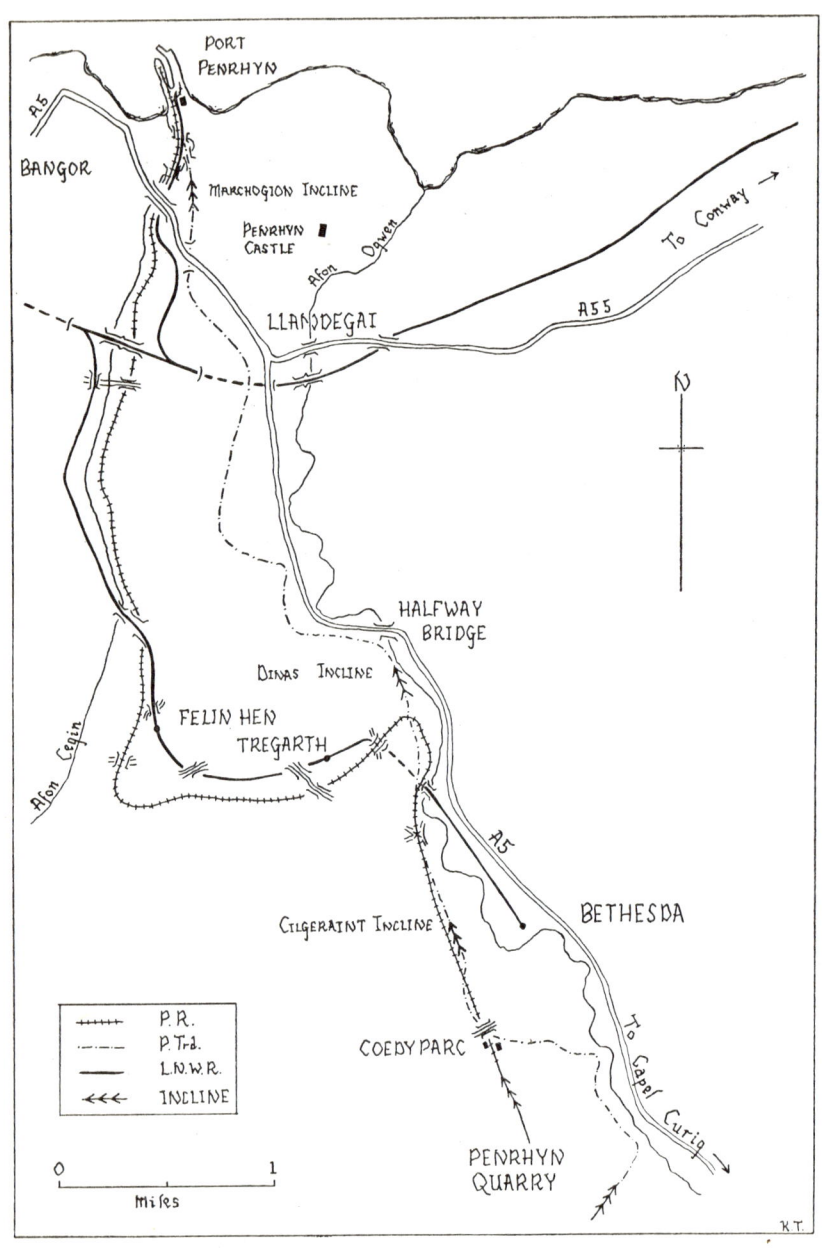

Map of the Penrhyn Railway and Tramroad

Page 51:
(above) *Padarn slate train at Penllyn, nearing the level crossing, just beyond the present terminus of the Llanberis Lake Railway;* (below) *Amalthaea on train of empties passing under the Bethel footbridge*

Page 52:
(left) *Padarn semaphore signal (Penscoins)*; (below) *Penscoins again: empty and loaded trains at the incline head. Note the guard's van on the rear of the loaded train*

THE PENRHYN RAILWAY 53

two sets of crossing gates were required. Additional protection came from a semaphore signal each side of the crossing, controlled from the keeper's hut. From here it occupied the tramroad route for ½ mile, fairly and squarely following the old course beside the road. As the road falls away below the railway so the trackbed clings to the hillside atop an ever-growing slate wall: the topmost section of this wall was built to protect the Penrhyn Railway; the division between it and the rest of the tramroad retaining wall below can still be clearly seen. This section of the line is scenically the most beautiful of the whole railway with the hillside on the left, the road below on the right and, far below that again, the rocky course of the Ogwen; the scene is completed by the shady trees that fill the valley and overhang the line.

Reaching the top of the Dinas incline the railway abruptly left the tramroad for an entirely different route. Here it turned through 180° in a hairpin bend to follow the land contours (and the edge of the wood) before crossing a minor road bridge and swinging away from its south-west direction to take a more westerly course. Here was the Penrhyn Railway's first bridge over the LNWR's branch to Bethesda after its completion in 1884 (opened 1 July). The standard gauge line had taken the opposite side of the narrow Ogwen valley from Bethesda before crossing the river and burrowing under the whole of the hairpin bend on the Penrhyn at Dinas in a ¼ mile tunnel; the Penrhyn crossed the branch immediately after its emergence from the tunnel. The line was now in the village of Tregarth, 2¾ miles from the quarry, and passed under what is now the B4366 road close to the LNWR branch. (The latter line had a station to serve the village.) Continuing for another ½ mile the Penrhyn reached its halfway passing loop, dived in a shallow cutting under a hump-back stone arch which carried a farm road over it and swung south-west then north in a long curve towards Felin Hen. On the inside of this curve was a trailing junction with a spur and two sidings into a small ballast 'quarry'.

At Felin Hen the B4366 was crossed again on another bridge before the railway began its descent into the peaceful valley

D

of the Cegin. Still it was parallel on its new northwards course by the LNWR line (a second intermediate station was sited at Felin Hen) until ½ mile from the village the Penrhyn joined the river and both were crossed by the standard gauge line. The railway then closely followed the Cegin the rest of the way to Port Penrhyn, passing with it under the Chester-Holyhead main line viaduct between the Bangor and Llandegai tunnels. The Bethesda branch, meanwhile, after its viaduct over the Penrhyn and the Cegin, steadily rose higher up the valley side to meet the main line. In the process it crossed one minor road which immediately forded the river and then rose to pass over the Penrhyn line.

As the line approached the port it dived under the A5 road and soon joined the tramroad route again, crossing the Cegin twice (first by a single arch bridge and then by a three arch bridge), before reaching the quayside. The steepest gradient on the new line was 1 in 37 for ¼ mile above the Hendurnpike crossing; three miles were graded at 1 in 40. The total drop was 550ft from quarry to port and the average gradient 1 in 91½. The sharpest curve was 85ft radius. Total length of the line was just over 6½ miles.

PORT PENRHYN

In 1810 the Rev J. Evans wrote:

Two miles from Bangor is ABER CEGID or CEGIN through which a small rivulet empties itself into the Menai. On this a new harbour is fast rising into consequence, formed at the expense of the late Lord Penrhyn, (and called after his name) for the advantage of his lordship's slate quarries which are four miles above at *Dolawyn*, near Llyn Meirig, in the mountains of Ogwen. The situation of Port Penrhyn is convenient, being well situated by the Anglesea shore, and vessels of three or four hundred tons burthen ride securely close to the quay to take in their lading; some of these are from London, Bristol, and Liverpool; but the chief trade is with Ireland. This is made the grand depot of the slate trade; and spacious warehouses are erected for that purpose. . . .

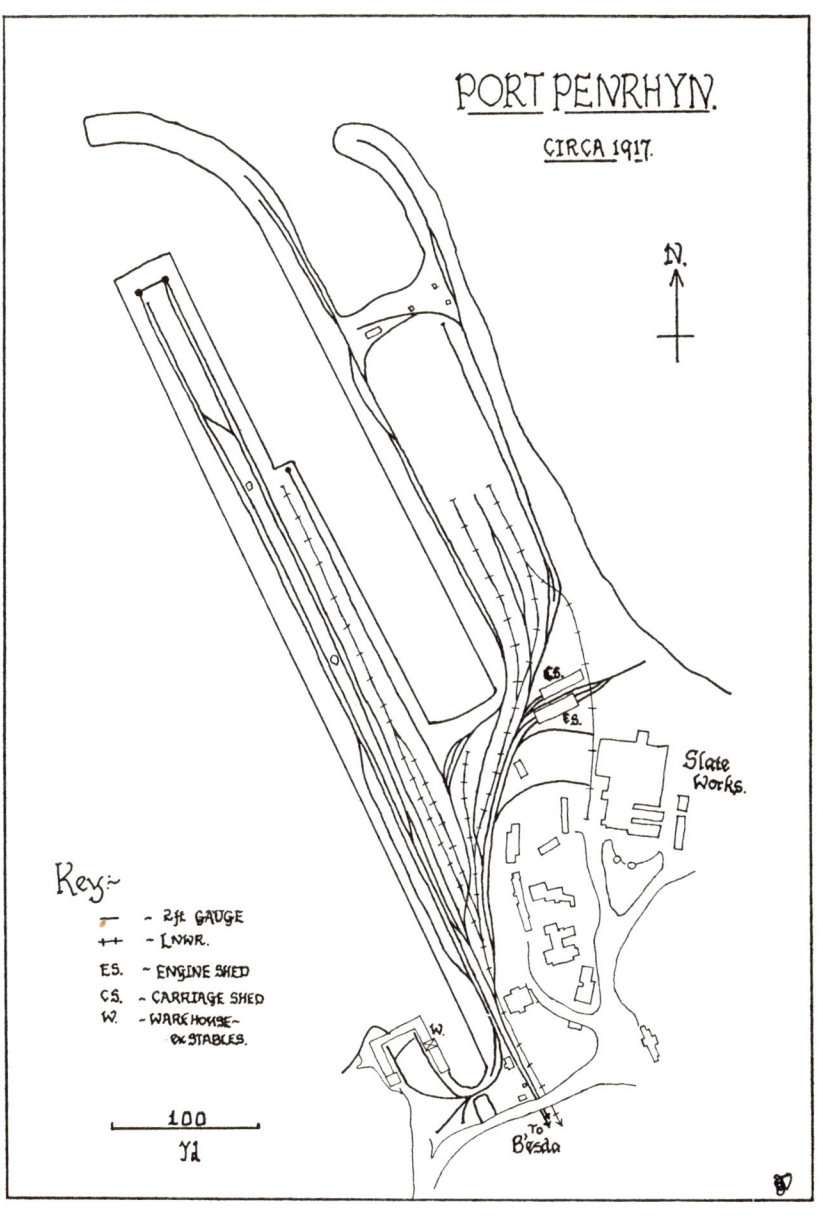

Thus wrote Evans of a port established twenty years previous by Richard Pennant. It had been improved beyond recognition by Evans' time. In 1794 just 1590 tons of slate were shipped from Port Penrhyn; in 1804 229 ships cleared out of the port whilst in 1844 it was recorded that 440 cargoes totalling 41,000 tons were shipped westwards, one vessel taking up to three cargoes. An unknown but equally large quantity was shipped eastwards. In 1838 Lewis wrote of 'a commodius wharf', spacious warehouses, ships of 300 tons and 200 men at work in the port. Each vessel carried a crew of about six men. The port itself consisted of a single quay, more than 1000ft long and capable of holding more than 100 trading ships, projecting into the Menai Straits; to the east of this jetty was situated a harbour for vessels awaiting cargoes. (This side of the port was known by those who worked there as 'White Man's Grave' on account of its non-existent protection from the elements!) This final layout of the port was the work of James Wyatt and since his day the basic design has not been altered.

As happened elsewhere in North Wales, the slate sailing ships gave way to the steamers; those working from Port Penrhyn belonged to the Anglesey Shipping Co, a company associated with the quarry. With the decline of the slate industry as a whole came the decline of the port, though even after the closure of the Penrhyn Railway in 1962 (see below) it was still occasionally used for shipments. (Port Dinorwic was also latterly used to export Penrhyn slates, in both cases these being taken from the quarry to the ports by road.) As recently as 1970 a cargo was shipped out to France when on 24 June the tramp steamer *Heather* sailed for St Malo laden with 400 tons of purple and pale grey crazy paving slabs.

### THE PORT PENRHYN BRANCH

The Port Penrhyn standard gauge branch was opened by the Chester & Holyhead Railway in 1852, this company having had the foresight to realise the pecuniary advantages and gains to be reaped from the broadening slate industry. It thus took the logical step of building a transhipment siding with the Penrhyn Railway. Equally logically, this was at Port Penrhyn. There was a trailing junction with the up main line (C & HR) just west of Llandegai tunnel with accompanying storage siding complete with signal box. This spot was officially known as Penrhyn Sidings. The branch left the sidings as a single track line through a gate and turned sharply northwards on a continually falling gradient (1 in 50 at its steepest point). After travelling ½ mile it converged with the Penrhyn Railway

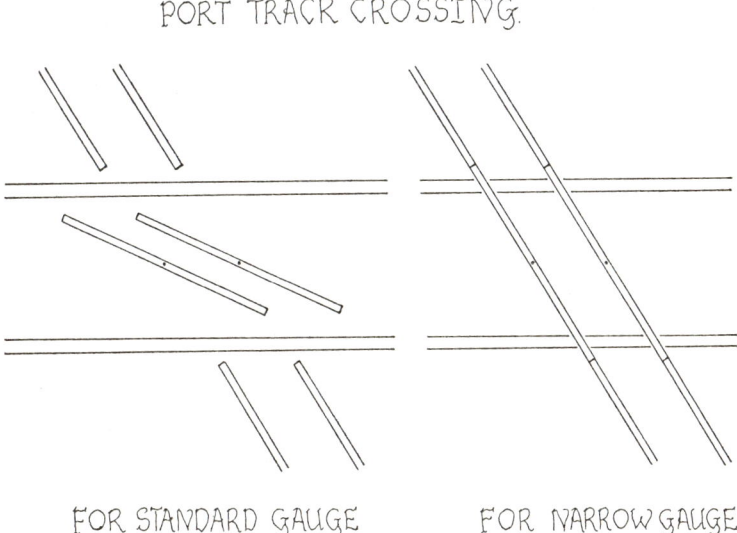

and ran along its eastern side under the Bangor-Chester main road (A5)—each had its own bridge since at this point, now having come ¾ mile, the standard gauge branch was still higher in the valley than the narrow gauge line. The tracks then ran inside the edge of the Penrhyn Castle Estate, both lines crossing the Cegin on a pile bridge. They soon recrossed the river on a three-arch wooden viaduct; then, passing under a minor road bridge (again, two separate arches) leading to the port from the A5, emerged on to the quay.

On the quay the narrow gauge lines crossed the standard

gauge sidings at various points on the level by the simple expedient of laying pivoted sections of narrow gauge rails across the standard gauge ones (see diagram). The only drawback was that occasionally LNWR locomotives fitted with water scoops would foul the narrow gauge rails! As it was a single line the branch was worked by a staff system with only one train allowed on the line at a time. Furthermore, this was only permitted at certain times of the day so that narrow gauge shunting could cease and the rail crossings set for standard gauge traffic. The waggon brakes would be pinned down at Penrhyn Sidings and the train of empties propelled down the branch by one or occasionally two engines. The driver had to sound his whistle all the way down while the guard rode on the leading waggon carrying a warning flag or lamp. Normal traffic consisted of one train in each direction (ie one load of empty and one of laden trucks) on weekdays only. The loaded waggons would be hauled up the branch in the usual manner. Other traffic consisted of coal for transhipment on to the Penrhyn Railway (to be taken up to the quarry to power machines there) and special bulk loads such as timber.

From 22 August 1954 the branch was reduced in status from a branch line to a siding and the Penrhyn Sidings box removed. Access to the branch (from the up line only) was now controlled by a ground frame electrically governed from the Bethesda Junction box. Trains bound for Bangor would back on to the up line and travel to Bethesda Junction under wrong line working procedure before being able to cross on to the down line. This arrangement lasted until 2 March 1963 when the whole branch followed the Penrhyn Railway into closure.

### WORKING

In October 1879 a total of 39 employees worked on the Penrhyn Railway. They comprised

1 Overlooker
9 Platelayers

## THE PENRHYN RAILWAY

    3 Port Platelayers
    6 Quarry Platelayers
    4 Engine Drivers
    4 Stockers [sic]
    2 Guards
    1 Flagman
    1 Signalman
    2 Gatemen
    1 Waggon Cleaner
    1 Quarry Oilman
    4 Port Oilmen
            (From quarry records)

By August 1890 the number was down to 30 men:
    1 Overlooker
    4 Foremen Platelayers
    1 Port Platelayer
    4 Quarry Platelayers
    5 Engine Drivers
    5 Stockers
    2 Brakemen
    1 Signalman
    2 Gatemen
    1 Quarry Oilman
    3 Port Oilmen
    1 Platelayer's Helper

At the quarry the dressed slates were loaded into main line slate waggons and let down the incline to Coed y Parc before being taken by one of the Penrhyn Railway engines to Port Penrhyn. These engines ran cab first down to the port. (As on the Padarn, there were no facilities for turning them.) At Port Penrhyn the slates were unloaded and stacked on the quayside while the empty waggons were taken back to the quarry. Apart from the matter of transporters, the Penrhyn Railway differed from the Padarn in one other important respect: whilst only Dinorwic slates were conveyed on the Padarn, other traffic was carried by the Penrhyn. These other commodities were, principally, fullersite (powdered slate), which was carried in bags in special waggons to the port and coal, carried in its own waggons from the port to the quarry. Here it was used to drive the quarry machinery not connected to the main water wheel and the locomotives there. Slate slabs were also brought down to the port on special waggons while timber and other long loads were taken up to the quarry on bolsters.

The railway was worked, as was the Padarn, on the one engine in steam principle. The engine in use was shedded at the port overnight. As on the Padarn, the railway also ran a quarrymen's train. At Penrhyn the service was operated by the men themselves by means of a society, set up for that specific purpose, to which they subscribed. This service first ran on 2 February 1879 and set the example for the more elaborate Padarn service to be described in the following chapters. The engine shedded at the port hauled the men to the quarry first thing in the morning between 6.00 am and 7.00 am (the locomotive being hired from the management for the occasion) and brought them home in the evening.

The Penrhyn had its own right-of-way, as had the Padarn: the most obvious difference between them though (apart from the gauge) was that whereas the Padarn Railway ran for the most part between stone and slate walls, the Penrhyn was fenced-off on the lower section in a manner equally common in North Wales: slate slabs upended in the ground and wired together at the top.

### QUARRY AND RAILWAY

In 1869 the Penrhyn Quarry produced 93,000 tons of roofing slates whilst in addition the production of slabs, writing slates etc was above 26,000 tons. The table below shows the production of roofing slates in the following years:

| | |
|---|---|
| 1870 | 91,700 tons |
| 1871 | 84,800 tons |
| 1872 | 85,500 tons |

By 1873 3500 men were hard at work in the quarry: all these figures are indicative of the reason behind the Penrhyn Railway's construction. A contemporary source states:

It has taken great efforts and the expenditure of large sums of money to develop both the Penrhyn and Dinorwig Quarries into regular galleries successfully worked, out of the inchoate mass of rubbish, heaps, and holes, left by former workers.

(Davies 1878)

George Sholto Gordon Douglas-Pennant succeeded his father in 1886 and began to take a great personal interest in the supervision of the quarry—an interest which was later to clash with those of his employees.

From its opening the railway was worked by 0-4-0 tank engines built by de Winton at Caernarvon. These were not apparently as powerful or as efficient as was desired and in 1882 Hunslets supplied a more powerful locomotive, *Charles*, for use on the line; this was a larger version of the basic type later widely used in the Penrhyn and Dinorwic Quarries. It was found to be a success and in 1893 two similar locomotives, *Blanche* and *Linda*, were supplied to work the railway. The de Wintons were then relegated to quarry duties. (Further details of the locomotives are given in Chapter 5.)

On Thursday, 12 July 1894 the Penrhyn Quarry was honoured by a visit from the Prince and Princess of Wales. They drove from Penrhyn Castle at noon, amidst banners and streamers; flags and cheering crowds lined the route. The quarrymen had a day's holiday in honour of the occasion. They lined the roadway, dressed in their holiday clothes of black coats and white corduroy trousers. In all there were 10,000 spectators. There had been no blasting in the quarry for three days but over 1500 charges had been laid and these went off in a succession of volleys. The royal couple then tried their hand at slate splitting, followed by the Bethesda Choir singing Welsh airs and the National Anthem. The party lunched in a marquee on the lawn of Ogwen Bank until 3.30 pm when they returned to Penrhyn Castle and Port Penrhyn where they toured the harbour in Lord Penrhyn's distinctive private railway carriage.

In this same year the rails on the Penrhyn Railway were lifted and replaced by 50lb bullhead rails which survived until the railway's closure. At this time 2950 men were employed in the quarry, a slight drop over preceding years, but output had risen to 110,000 tons per annum—an amount necessitating the removal of some 1,400,000 tons of waste rock. Soon Douglas-Pennant's strict supervision of the working of the quarry led to clashes with the men on account of his anti-unionist stand. Consequently, unlike Dinorwic where the management recognised the new trends within the industry, Penrhyn suffered drastically through Lord Penrhyn's unbending attitude. The history of the whole period of dispute is outside the scope of this book but two events need to be mentioned for their effect upon the railway. First, from September 1896 to August 1897 there was a complete strike lasting for a total of 270 working days. Second, there then followed the great lockout which began in 1900 and lasted for no less than three whole years, though for the latter part of this period the quarry was worked at 45% capacity by non-unionists. Douglas-Pennant's death came (perhaps timely for the future of the quarry) in 1907 and he was succeeded by his son Edward Sholto Douglas-Pennant, the third Lord Penrhyn. Relations with the men improved but, as at Dinorwic, the quarry was not helped by the fact that it lost so many men during World War I. In 1927 Edward Sholto's son Hugh Napier Douglas-Pennant succeeded to the estate as the fourth Lord Penrhyn.

In 1923 an attempt was made to acquire additional locomotives for use on the railway and in fact three had been purchased. These were Baldwins which had been built for use in France by the US Army during World War I and were afterwards going cheap. They were not a good bargain by any means (no doubt because they were constructed in a hurry and only intended for brief war service) as the individual details given in Chapter 5 will show. After a short period of work on the Penrhyn Railway they were withdrawn and eventually disposed of in 1940.

The same problems dealt with in the next chapter in relation to the Dinorwic Quarry also applied to Penrhyn. Britain's imports of slate had risen from a few hundred tons before

1890 to 20,000 tons in 1895 and to a staggering 120,000 tons per annum just eight years later. The fact that in 1937 imports were down to 25,670 tons is indicative of the falling demand for slates rather than increased home production. In that same year of 1937 employment had fallen to 1916—below that at Dinorwic—and short-time working was normal. Both the quarry and the railway were in a bad way (in August 1940 the quarry had to be closed for nine weeks owing to a shortage of men) and despite a brief post-World War II boom it was obvious that with Lord Penrhyn's death in 1949 the old order had come to an end.

### CLOSURE

After Lord Penrhyn's death Penrhyn Castle and 40,000 acres of land were forfeited to pay death duties; two years later it was conveyed to the National Trust. On 9 February of that same year, 1951, the workmen's passenger service ceased on the railway. In January 1952 the quarry was taken over by a company known as Penrhyn Quarries Ltd which continued to operate the railway, exclusively steam worked to the last, in the face of rising maintenance costs, falling traffic and increased competition from road haulage. It lasted ten years before finally succumbing on 24 July 1962. The track was not lifted until 1965 when the rails were sold to the Festiniog Railway—which had already acquired two of the railway's three surviving locomotives (*Blanche* and *Linda*). The Bethesda-Bangor standard gauge branch soon followed the way of the Penrhyn Railway when it closed on 6 October 1963 (it had already been closed to passenger traffic from 3 December 1951), although the Bethesda Junction signal box survived until 1 August 1965 after the closure of the Port Penrhyn branch.

Meanwhile the National Trust was planning turning part of Penrhyn Castle into an industrial locomotive museum. This was carried out and the Penrhyn Railway's third locomotive, *Charles*, was sent there. The museum officially opened on 25 June 1965. Two years earlier there had been a move to form a preservation society either to buy or lease the remains of the railway, with a view to operating it after the necessary restoration work on both track and locomotives, but this had come to nothing.

CHAPTER 4

## *The Padarn Railway*

### THE DINORWIC TRAMROAD

The Dinorwic Tramroad was not constructed until 13 years after that at Penrhyn—probably because of the lesser volume of slate transported. However, from 1824 onwards it began its seven mile journey close to the village of Dinorwic, some 1000ft above sea level. From here it was linked to the separate Allt Ddu workings and by a tramroad known as the Village Tramway to the Mills section of the Dinorwic Quarry. It commenced its run in a north-easterly direction for one mile before dropping 500ft in ¼ mile down two successive inclines (still remarkably well preserved) to the village of Deiniolen. Here it crossed a small stream, the Caledd Ffrwd. The route then levelled out, a broad, comparatively level coastal plain spreading before it, and took a more northerly course which brought it close to what is now the B4547 road. By now it had covered over four miles of its more or less straight-ahead journey. The track then ran down from the plateau, crisscrossing the road as it wound through the narrow valley east of Port Dinorwic (a third incline was needed near the head of the valley by which it descended) until one mile from the port itself it turned sharply westwards, crossing the fields beside the Bangor road. By the time it reached its destination it had covered seven miles and dropped 1000ft—an average gradient (excluding the inclines) of roughly 1 in 40.

Little is known about the working of the tramroad—which

is hardly surprising in view of its short life. Presumably the quarry waggons were used, drawn by horses, though considering the steepness of the line it is very likely that gravity working was also in force. The three inclines were double and presumably self-acting, based on those in the quarry. In view of the fact that the same gauge was used (and in the quarry) as that at Penrhyn, and that the whole line was modelled on the example set by Penrhyn, it is more than probable that the permanent way was much the same as that used on the Penrhyn Tramroad. The early form of permanent way later adopted for the new Padarn Railway would also indicate that the method of laying the rails in chairs spiked to stone blocks was carried over from the tramroad.

### DINORWIC QUARRY

The years 1825-50 were to see a revolutionary improvement in production methods at Dinorwic: tools were improved and mechanisation introduced while safety fuses made blasting safer and dynamite began to replace the old black powder. Even so, slate quarrying was a hazardous profession and serious accidents—and often fatalities—were literally an everyday occurrence. The new tramroad was not to last the quarter-century though at the start the era was well under way with the line to the port in full use and the tracks linked to it spreading rapidly throughout the quarry. These changes, though, were not always easily accomplished.

In 1825 there was a minor revolt in the quarry when the general manager, Mr William Turner, introduced a new code of rules and regulations. Among other things it stated that work was to cease at 4.00 pm on Saturdays and not at 1.00 pm as had been usual. On the first day this was put into effect Turner and the head overseer stalwartly placed themselves at the quarry exit, but to no avail: at 1.00 pm the quarrymen simply trotted past them, smiles on their faces. The quarrymen won the issue. A year later the quarry had over 800 men working it and production had reached 20,000 tons a year—and for every ton of slate produced between 12 and 20 tons of waste rock had to be removed. Profits reached a new record but this was short lived; by 1827 Dinorwic and the other quarries were all carrying large stocks of slate because of a reduction in demand. From July 1827 until the spring of 1831 slate prices fell progressively and for several years the industry worked very much below its full productive capacity.

Assheton-Smith had an excellent plan for encouraging good conduct and integrity amongst his workmen during this period. He began a system of allotting portions of the mountain land on his estate to the most deserving workmen; the selection was based on merit and the decision left to the quarry manager. Between fifteen and twenty acres would be meted out at a nominal rent on the understanding that the quarryman was to build a cottage for himself and his family. In this way, by the 1850s, nearly 2000 acres of land were brought under continuous cultivation—land originally covered by bracken and heather. The occupiers were allowed to sell their holdings to their fellow labourers if they so wished but this was rarely done. Thomas Assheton-Smith died in 1828 and was succeeded by his son, also named Thomas, who had been Conservative member for Andover since 1821. From 1832 to 1841 he sat for Caernarvonshire before being succeeded by Douglas-Pennant.

As has been mentioned earlier, the slate duty was repealed in 1831 and in the decade following this the population of Caernarvonshire increased by 22%, almost twice the rate for any other county in North Wales. In the first half of the nineteenth century the export trade was small but it was growing and shipments were being sent regularly to the United States of America (indeed 17,782 tons were shipped there in 1831) and occasionally to the Continent. In 1842 the foreign market received a boost when there was a serious fire at Hamburg, which suffered extensive damage; naturally new buildings required new roofs and this meant more Dinorwic slate was called for—such was its international reputation. In 1848 1600 men were employed at the quarry, making an overall total of 10,000 people, including the workers at the port and all the families, supported by the quarry. At this time, because of the rapid population growth, the old village of Llanberis (Nant Peris) became depopulated in favour of a new Llanberis which was established on the southern shore of Llyn Padarn closer to the quarry.

## A NEW LINE IS BUILT

In view of the Dinorwic Quarry's continuing expansion, in terms of both output and sheer physical size, it was decided in 1841 that a new tramroad was needed to link the quarry and the port. This was to commence at a lower point on the mountainside than the 1824 line since it was more efficient to lower slate to the bottom of the quarry workings than it would be to lift it from the lower galleries to the old tramroad. Thus it was decided to start the new line at the very edge of Llyn Padarn and from there travel by an entirely new route to Port Dinorwic. Here an incline was necessitated from the back of the village, through a short tunnel under the Bangor-Caernarvon road and out on to the quayside.

The rest of the story is nowhere near as simple. A new gauge of 4ft was chosen for the tramroad; this in turn was the reason behind the Port Dinorwic incline since in theory, once on the coastal plateau, the new route could easily have converged with the old and followed the latter's course (and existing incline). This idea was ruled out—at the expense of constructing the new incline—in favour of a broader, virtually level track. The obvious reason is, of course, that locomotive haulage was envisaged—or so one assumes until it is discovered that stables were constructed along the line at various points and until 1848 there is no evidence whatever that steam traction was intended. It must also be remembered that the adoption of a wider gauge meant that a greater proportion of slate could be included in the load hauled by a single horse. Whether the line was planned from the start as a steam railway or whether everything fell into place coincidentally, the abandonment of the original tramroad after so few years and its replacement with a locomotive-worked railway was without precedent in North Wales.

Page 69:
(above) Jenny Lind *in her later years*: note the added cab. (The poor quality of this photograph is outweighed by the fact that it is the only known one of a Padarn Horlock locomotive in service); (below) Amalthaea *on a workman's train at Gilfach Ddu. The structure on the right is the covered platform/carriage shed*

Page 70:
(above) *Hardy petrol locomotive at Gilfach Ddu;*
(right) *Padarn platelayers' bogie preserved at Gilfach Ddu in the slate museum;*
(below) *Assheton-Smith's private saloon*

The construction of the new line was undertaken on the 'bargain' system of a large number of contracts for relatively small amounts of work. This was the method used for working the quarry and it is not surprising that it was carried outside those confines. In all, 136 contractors, all local firms and none probably representing more than half-a-dozen men, were given 247 contracts between June 1841 and November 1842. In the main these were for the levelling of so many yards of ground, blasting so much rock away, building such and such a length of breast wall, constructing a road bridge; in short, preparing the track bed along the route, working simultaneously from a number of points. A large number of the contracts also included or comprised the procuring and drilling of stone blocks at 16s a dozen for laying the rails on. A fewer number were awarded to local iron foundries and blacksmiths for the construction of large slate waggons.

The main permanent way contractor appears to have been one William Foulke. On 26 November 1841 he was paid 10s for repairing 41½yd of rails, though exactly what this means is unclear. On 18 February 1842 he was given a contract for raising an unspecified amount of sleepers and temporary rails, presumably so as to lay the permanent track. (The temporary track was almost certainly of 1ft 10¾in gauge.) Another of Foulke's contracts (4 March 1842) is recorded in the book of contracts as 'Unloading Iron Rails from Waggons at Glanybala, Penllyn & Pontrhythallt for 6d a Ton: (367 Tons)'. Some at least of the rails had been laid by 23 July 1842 for on that date a contract was issued for cutting a drain between them at Cefn; on 14 September of that same year one contractor was paid for using 18 more blocks whilst laying rails than had first been calculated.

The permanent way consisted of stone blocks (many of which had been shipped from Llanberis up Llyn Padarn by boat) at regular intervals upon which were fastened, by means of oak 'treenails', cast iron chairs. Into each chair the rail ends were secured with wooden keys; the rails themselves were of fish-bellied wrought iron pattern, 12ft long. No cross ties of any sort were used and the whole was ballasted with broken stone.

E

Apart from the fact that by the end of December 1843 the total bill for constructing and equipping the railway had amounted to £35,952 12s 6½d little is known about the first five years of its life. In 1848 two steam locomotives were purchased for the line from Horlock & Co of Northfleet, Kent. They were named *Jenny Lind* and *Fire Queen*, the latter also being the name of Assheton-Smith's private steam yacht. (Further information regarding these engines and the working of the line is given in Chapter 6.) Found to be unsuitable for heavy locomotives, the tramroad-style track was later relaid with wooden sleepers, cast iron chairs and 80lb per yard steel bullhead rails, to form a more conventional permanent way. By now the railway had been officially named the Dinorwic Quarry Railway, a name which it kept right through to the end of its life, though originally and always unofficially it was simply known as the Padarn Railway.

At an unknown early date the original waggons were scrapped and new vehicles introduced. These were transporter waggons and each carried four of the narrower gauge quarry waggons from the quarry to the Port Dinorwic incline where they were unloaded and lowered down to the quay. This means of conveyance formed the sole method of transporting slate over the railway throughout the remainder of its history.

### THE ROUTE DESCRIBED

From the quarry to the port incline the Padarn Railway was slightly less than seven miles in length. It started from a point at the south-east corner of Llyn Padarn, opposite Llanberis, where the slate waggons were loaded on to their transporters. This terminus was known as Gilfach Ddu and was situated inside the quarry works' yard; a later addition was a covered platform used as a carriage shed during the day. From here the line ran north-west, leaving Gilfach Ddu yard to hug the lake shore literally at the water's edge, through the Padarn valley between the mountains with the foothills of Elidir Fawr immediately to its right. From 1869 it was paralleled on the opposite side of the lake by the LNWR branch to Llanberis,

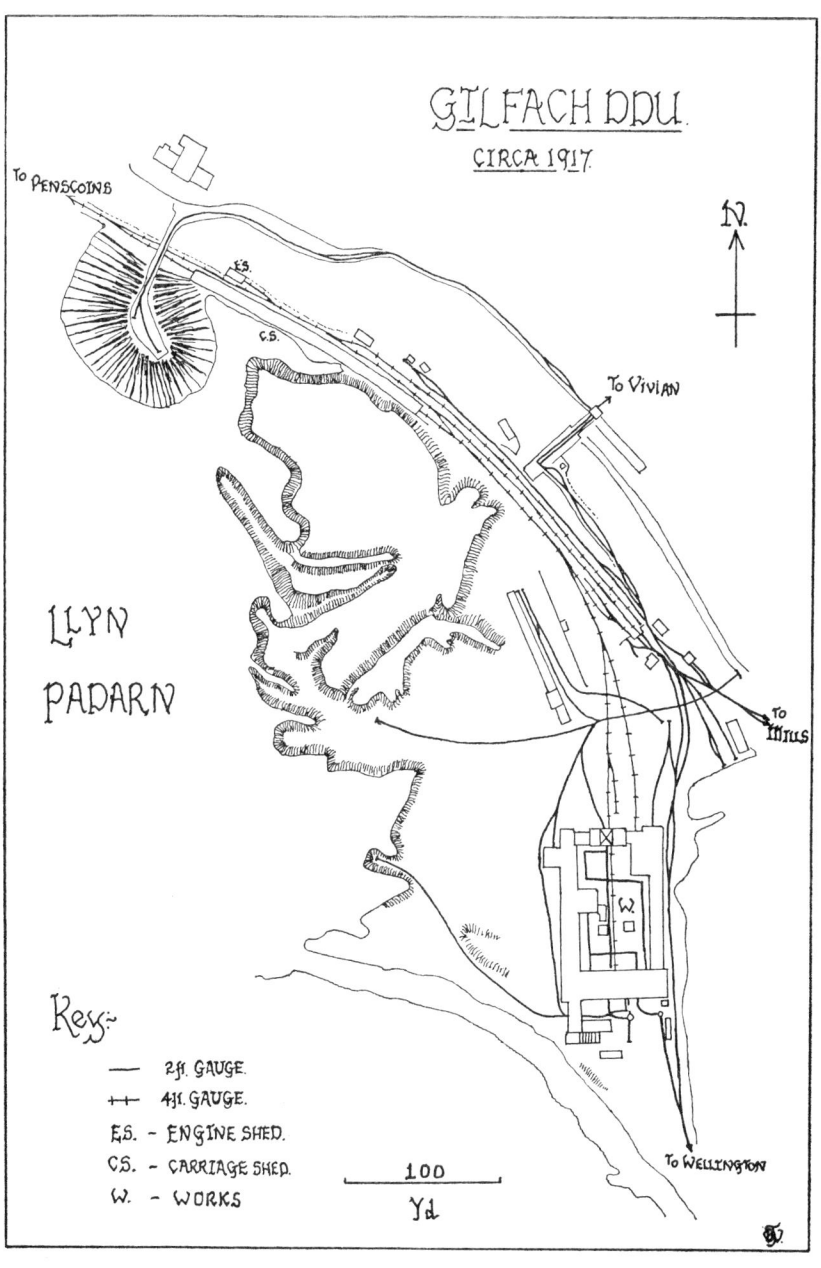

opened on 1 July 1869. The standard gauge branch was closed by the LMS on 22 September 1930, reopened 18 July 1932 and closed for the last time on 7 September 1962. Nearing the end of the lake it passed, via a level crossing, over a minor road and then under the B4547 at Penllyn. (An 1895 plan, never implemented, to do away with the crossing by diverting road and railway slightly would have avoided at least one accident.) This was the first stopping place for the quarrymen's train and had a four-coach platform. It was situated at the end of Llyn Padarn just over two miles from the quarry. The track continued north-westwards, still paralleled by the LNWR line across the Afon Rhythallt, through the pleasant wooded river valley, to Pontrhythallt (passing the second halt at Stabla in the process) a further 1¼ miles from Penllyn. Just before the ten-coach platform was a trailing junction leading to a long carriage shed. All this way the railway had roughly followed the 350ft contour.

At Pontrhythallt the bridge spanned the river and both the narrow and standard gauge railways; here the LNWR line crossed the river and joined the Padarn for a further ¾ mile before diverging westwards to follow the river—now known as the Afon Saint—to the sea at Caernarvon. The Padarn meanwhile continued in a more northerly direction, rising from the valley and up a long embankment over a minor road bridge. It then crossed another minor road on the level (315ft above sea level), bearing right to the Bethel level crossing—the scene of the only major accident in the line's history—and passing well to the east of the village. This was the fourth stopping place for the Dinorwic quarrymen's train, complete with a 152ft long platform on the left of the line (all the railway's stone and slate platforms were sited on this side of the line) and a trailing junction to a siding into the second carriage shed. Shortly before the station an impressive and unusual stone footbridge over the line allowed pedestrians using a footpath to cross the track.

Passing the Bethel platform, the railway crossed what is now the B4366 main Llandegai-Caernarvon road and ran north-north-east in a straight line from the crossing, passing Saron,

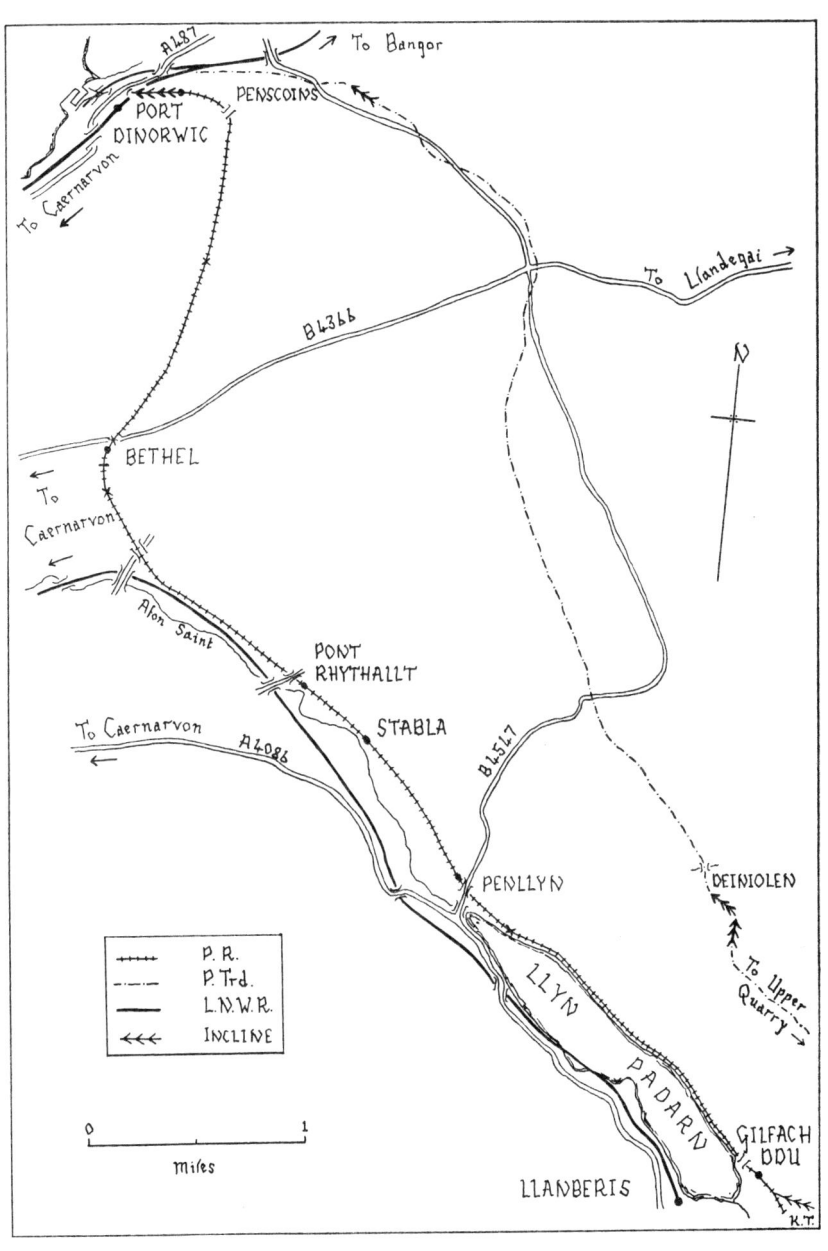

Map of the Padarn Railway and Tramroad

the village adjoining Bethel, on its left. It then passed over its fourth and final level crossing before running in a northerly direction to the back of Port Dinorwic, 1½ miles from Bethel, before curving sharply west. Diving under another minor road it ran immediately in front of a short row of cottages at Penscoins, the site of the railway's engine shed and final stopping place for the returning workmen, before it reached the unloading bay, 250ft above Port Dinorwic, at the head of the incline down to the quayside.

YEARS OF PROSPERITY—AND DISPUTE

The quarry continued to thrive in the 1850s and 1860s. During the latter years 100,000 tons of slate per annum were being produced and conveyed over the new railway; the 1856 figures show that Dinorwic was making a clear profit of £30,000 annually for its owner. The *Mining Journal* of 9 September 1859 gives the annual net profit as having reached £70,000! Thomas Assheton-Smith had died in 1858, passing the property on in his family, and at his death his 47,000 acre Welsh estates (excluding mountain land) exceeded £40,000 in value per annum—in addition to the slate revenue. In 1867 the export trade grew because of a widening European market whilst trade with the USA slackened. The position of the quarry was so strong that it was in a position to dictate terms to the merchants and was able to add 5 per cent to prices for all quantities of less than 30 tons sent by rail; no orders for less than 15 tons were executed.

By 1873 demand for slate had once again outstripped production and available supply while the quarry's productive capacity was hampered by long labour disputes. In December of that year steps were taken to form a quarrymen's union. It met weekly until early 1874 when it was decided to form a union for all the quarrymen in Caernarvonshire and Merionethshire. It was to be non-militant and known as the Society for the Defence of Slate Quarrymen, although the name was soon changed to that of the North Wales Quarrymen's Union. The first official meeting was held on 27 April 1874 at Caernarvon and was attended by representatives from the four chief slate-producing districts of North Wales. Assheton-Smith opposed all such activities and on 4 June announced that only non-unionists would be employed at Dinorwic. At the monthly letting of the bargains at the quarry on 18 June 2800 union men were 'locked out'. The men had no argument with the owner: they were happy with their wages, conditions and the management—they were appealing merely for the recognition of the union. A deputation of men met Assheton-Smith and the manager, Col Wyatt, to make it known that the union had been established simply for the men's protection and not for any aggressive or political purpose, or with the intention of interfering with the actual running of the quarry—or any other quarries in North Wales for that matter.

The management made the men an offer which was that a union, with Assheton-Smith as patron, would be formed, called the Dinorwic Quarries Union. All other officials and conditions were to be chosen by the men. It was suggested that there should be monthly subscriptions collected to help members, assist emigration, improve conditions and give aid to widows, orphans and the sick.

Nothing was agreed. Assheton-Smith refused recognition of the workers' union and the workers outrightly refused to accept a suggestion of what they believed to be little more than a Quarry Club. Early in July 1874 the Penrhyn quarrymen made a collection of £206 in support of the Dinorwic men. Lord Penrhyn objected and when the Penrhyn Lodge was established on 20 July 2300 men flocked to join the NWQU—this meeting was to result in the Penrhyn strike of 30 July 1874. After a lock-out of nearly five weeks the Dinorwic men returned to work on 20 July, having succeeded in persuading Assheton-Smith to employ them as unionists with all the union officials, except the secretary, quarrymen or other quarry employees.

1876 and 1877 were boom years (in fact the most prosperous ever experienced by the company); the Dinorwic and the Nantlle concerns took this splendid opportunity to raise their prices 20% above Penrhyn's, such was the demand for slate.

However, the inevitable happened and the demand declined, leaving the quarries with huge stocks which they could not get rid of. Dinorwic took the initiative and immediately reduced its prices, forcing the smaller concerns to cut theirs, and so it continued in one large, vicious circle. The slate industry was heading towards a crisis and the exploitation of the financial situation by the big companies was forcing many of the smaller producers to close down. In 1882 limited companies produced only 35,891 tons of slate against 244,825 tons from other organisations, making a total output of 280,716 tons for that year. Of those 'other organisations', Dinorwic and Penrhyn together produced no less than 198,595 tons of slate, valued at £468,212, with a work force of 5566 men. But in spite of this apparent prosperity for the two big concerns a general feeling of instability and insecurity prevailed; by this time the export growth was ending—other countries were also exporting slate and the building boom in Britain was in danger of becoming a slump.

The Dinorwic Quarry was determined to obtain a fair share of any profits going in the market and abandoned altogether its policy of consulting Penrhyn over uniform prices, instead producing an independent price list. With fluctuating demand this was felt to be a means of holding a steady share of the market. Indeed demand was falling so rapidly that the management found it necessary to reduce prices as low as possible *and* make additional concessions such as heavy discount rates and the sale of best quality slates at the price of inferior quality. As soon as particular sizes of slates began to accumulate in large quantities in the quarry the management was forced to dispose of them at far below the normal market price. Competition was keen and each quarry accused the others of undercutting or resorting to unsavoury means of gaining a larger share of the market. In the twenty years from 1862 to 1882 the output of the Dinorwic Quarry had fallen overall from 98,000 to 87,000 tons.

The management was also harassed by internal troubles. From 31 October 1885 to 1 March 1886 Dinorwic underwent a prolonged lock-out which temporarily reduced the supply of slates and caused prices to rise suddenly and drastically. This at least had its compensations for the small concerns which had been working at a steady loss for some years. The situation at Dinorwic became critical since the quarry proprietor could ill afford the dispute in terms of lost sales. More important was the effect of a working stoppage on the quarry itself: machinery left unmanned would suffer and the quarry would become generally neglected and derelict if left unattended for more than a short period. The same, of course, applied to the railway which was similarly affected by the dispute. Some work was resumed but this was merely unremunerative maintenance work done by overseers.

And as if all this was not enough, at the same time heavy capital expenditure was incurred by the purchase of two new locomotives for the railway. The old Horlock engines were outmoded and ailing and consequently replacements were ordered from the Hunslet Engine Co of Leeds—a firm which had given every satisfaction with its engines employed on the narrow gauge quarry lines (see Chapters 5 and 7). By comparison with the Horlocks the Hunslets were far more compact and powerful—and reliable. The first, appropriately named *Dinorwic*, was delivered in 1882 and the second, *Pandora*, four years later. The Horlocks were withdrawn and the new 0-6-0 tank engines took over their duties, apparently without incident.

### TWO ROYAL VISITS

In 1899 the Duke and Duchess of York visited the Dinorwic Quarry and their arrival at Llanberis from Llanrwst on Thursday 27 April was the subject of much enthusiasm. Descending into the village by carriage down Llanberis Pass, the distinguished party found their arrival awaited by the whole neighbourhood. The approach to the quarry was gaily decorated with streamer arches, as was the Padarn Railway at Gilfach Ddu in the works complex. Here and there on the galleries flags floated in the breeze. On both sides of the bridge on the road leading to the quarry between Llyn Peris and Llyn

Padarn, and for a considerable distance beyond, the children of the Llanberis Board School waited eagerly for a glimpse of the royal party. With the exception of a small number of men detailed for absolutely necessary duties the quarrymen ceased work at mid-day.

The actual time of the royals' arrival was not known and the spectators were taken unaware when the word went round that the royal carriage had been sighted. Two or three minutes later the party was nearing the quarry, saluted with the National Anthem by the little ones on the bridge. The equipage came to a standstill in the open space by the Padarn Railway, in front of Glanybala, the residence of one of the quarry agents, in the grounds of which a luncheon tent had been erected. In view of a large crowd, the royal guests were officially received by the Hon Walter W. Vivian, the quarry manager. They then climbed the steep and narrow red baize-covered path to the luncheon tent. A few minutes later those of the royal party who had travelled from Llanrwst by train arrived at the scene from Port Dinorwic in a Padarn Railway train composed of Assheton-Smith's private saloon and the quarrymen's carriage U; the identity of the locomotive is not recorded.

At 2.40 pm a thrill of excitement passed through the crowd as one of the quarry locomotives steamed up to the improvised platform at the reception area. The little engine was smartly set-off in front and behind with trophies and had a train of five passenger carriages. The royal party seated themselves and the train set off towards the Wellington area of the quarry. Here the visitors alighted to witness some slate dressing operations conducted by some half-dozen quarrymen. During their $\frac{1}{4}$ hour stay at this spot the party watched with interest the operations of the rock drilling machinery and the splitting and dressing of slates. Both the duke and duchess handled a chisel and separated two or three partly-split slates—an accomplishment of which they seemed exceedingly proud, particularly as it elicited expressions of approval from the rest of the party! They carried away with them a number of slates as a memento of the occasion.

The train then continued on its way, through a short tunnel, to the Hafod Owen section of the quarry where, at the end of the line, the engine was detached and the train split into two portions. Both were then drawn up the inclines to the California Gallery (C3A). The train was remarshalled, a new locomotive attached and the travellers taken along the side of the mountain towards the work face. At a junction with the permanent gallery track the locomotive was uncoupled and its place taken by some of the gentlemen passengers and some quarrymen. After travelling a short distance over the lighter temporary track the party halted by a hut from which they were to witness a blasting operation specially staged for their benefit. The spectacle was an impressive one—the whole valley resounded—and was regarded with great admiration by all. The guests then proceeded upon their way along the California Gallery into the A4A level where they descended the successive inclines at the other side of the quarry, finally arriving at the bottom at Gilfach Ddu. Here they were greeted by a large crowd of people, conspicuous among whom were the members of the Caernarvon Cycling Club standing in a proud line by their machines.

The royal party then boarded the Padarn Railway special train (complete with bedecked engine) and departed for Port Dinorwic amidst loud cheers. Alighting at Penscoins they proceeded down the incline to the point where it crossed the LNWR Bangor-Caernarvon line. Here Mr Dawson, the LNWR district engineer, had had erected a temporary platform to enable the party to reach the royal train which had arrived from Llanwrst earlier in the day. They had a splendid reception from the huge crowd of spectators while the Port Dinorwic Juvenile Choir sang some Welsh songs and, of course, the National Anthem. Assheton-Smith's daughter Enid presented the Duke of York with a buttonhole of white flowers attached to a gold pin and the departure for Llanwrst was then hastily made just as a heavy shower began. So ended the first royal visit.

The second visit took place on 17 May 1902 when the as yet uncrowned King Edward VII and Queen Alexandra visited the quarry on an ideal day of unclouded sunshine. As on the occasion three years before, flags and streamers brightened the uniform tint of the hillside as they fluttered in the breeze. The King and Queen, accompanied by Mr and Mrs Assheton-Smith, drove from Vaynol to Llanberis along the main road via Caernarvon; large numbers of people cheered heartily as they lined the route. Just before 4.00 pm the party arrived at the quarry where a guard of honour was inspected by the Queen. Then, as on the occasion of the first royal visit, the guests were taken in passenger carriages up the inclines to a suitable vantage point from which to witness a blast in the Matilda department of the quarry, ½ mile distant. The purpose of the blast was to join the Garret and Diphwys Galleries into one. Contrary to normal practice no holes had had to be drilled in the rock for the explosive: a huge natural crevice already existed in the rock and into this had been poured no less than 2½ tons of gunpowder. Mrs Assheton-Smith handed to the Queen a little slate casket in which there lay a key; with the key the Queen opened a box on the temporary platform within which was a button. She pressed the button and this electrically caused a fuse to be lit, the length of which was so calculated that the spark took six minutes to reach the explosive. When the moment arrived the rock was hurled forward in a veritable shower of fragments and the explosion emitted a dark cloud of smoke which ascended balloon-like to the sky whilst from below there slowly rose a tremendous volume of dust caused by the falling debris. The operation was carried out with perfect success and resulted in the removal of 50-60,000 tons of rock, a large proportion of which was later used for slates. After the blast the whole party went to inspect the result and was rewarded with the sight of a second fall.

A male voice choir ended a programme of music for the royal visitors who, having partaken of tea in a room in the quarry foundry, journeyed back to Port Dinorwic via the Padarn Railway. They spent Sunday at Vaynol before leaving the next day. In June of that same year the King fell very ill and a particularly heavy gloom was cast over Llanberis. His coronation was postponed. Eventually cheerful news concerning his health was received and a huge bonfire was lit in celebration on 30 June on the very spot where the Queen had fired the blast on her visit to the quarry. A huge crowd collected to witness the blaze.

PORT DINORWIC

In his *Topographical Dictionary of Wales* (1838 Vol II) Samuel Lewis describes the port thus:

> Port Dinorwig a small port in the parish of Llanvairis gaer hundred of ISGORVAL, county of Caernarvon, North Wales three and a half miles North North East from Caernarvon: the population is returned with the parish. This place anciently called "Aber Pwll" is situated on the Menai Straits and has a small but commodious harbour, accessible at high waters to vessels of hundred tons burden.

In fact the site was more usually known (as today in Welsh), as Y Felin Heli, meaning The Saltwater Mill, after an old mill that had been turned by the ebbing tide.

The port was close to the Vaynol park and had grown out of a natural harbour formed by the mouth of a small stream, beautifully situated in the very centre of the straits, equidistant from the open sea at Caernarvon Bay and Puffin Island. A more colourful description of its position (somewhat inaccurate as regards the Marquis of Anglesey's column) is given in *Reminiscences of the Late Thomas Assheton Smith Esq* by Sir Herbert Maxwell in 1859:

> From an eminence above the port can be seen the magnificent structure of Stephenson and Telford's elegant and graceful work. Opposite is the pillar erected to commemorate the gallantry of one of the bravest of the house of Paget. To the left as the traveller gazes up the straits in the direction of Orme's Head, is the pretty town of Beaumaris, and immediately above it the extensive woods encircling the noble mansion of Baron Hill.

Like Port Penrhyn, Port Dinorwic was a private port used only for the shipment of slates from its associated quarry. (The name later came to include the village that grew up around it.) It was begun on a small scale by Thomas Assheton-Smith's father, but on the son's accession in 1828 it was enlarged and extended. He also added two sets of dock gates, one behind the other, in the former creek and by 1838 it was large enough to hold thirty vessels; twenty years later it could accommodate securely 120 ships alongside the quays, in the harbour or in the dock, all sheltered from the wind. A branch of the former Bangor & Caernarvon Railway connected it with the Chester & Holyhead Railway (see below) by which means slates could be conveyed in large quantities to the manufacturing and urban districts of Britain. At this time slates were shipped to most seaports of England, Ireland, Scotland, the Baltic, Germany and extensively to the USA.

In the early years of the nineteenth century shipping had been more primitive and the amount shipped much smaller. The slate had left the port in small vessels bound mainly for Liverpool or Ireland. The industry was very little affected even by the Napoleonic Wars, passing through these virtually unscathed. Trade to America began to develop: in April 1817 the *Chester Chronicle* was able to report the loading of three large ships, two at Port Dinorwic and one at Port Penrhyn, with slates for North America. Exports were increasing and in 1844 44,881 tons of slate were shipped eastwards; in that same year a total of 653 vessels laden with slates left Port Dinorwic for various parts of the world. By 1850 the joint tonnage exported from the three leading slate ports of Port Dinorwic, Port Penrhyn and Portmadoc (Caernarvon had by now lost its supremacy) had reached about 200,000 tons annually. Despite the coming of the railways during the 1850s and 1860s the port was still crammed with vessels—in 1866 no fewer than 764 left its harbour, an average of more than two loaded and cleared out every day of the year. As late as 1895 339 vessels carried slate from Port Dinorwic.

By now steamers were replacing the old sailing ships and the Dinorwic Quarry owned its own small fleet of these. One unfortunate incident mars their almost unblemished history. In the early hours of the morning of Saturday, 11 October 1902 (a clear night), the cargo steamer *Vaynol*, 200 tons burden, bound from Glasgow to Port Dinorwic, was somehow run into by the Grimsby steam trawler *Lucerne* between the Mull of Galloway and the Manx coast. The *Lucerne's* bow cut right into the engine room of the *Vaynol* and the latter boat immediately began to flounder. Fortunately the crew of nine were picked up by the trawler. After landing them at Port Erin the badly damaged *Lucerne* proceeded to Barrow for repairs.

Before World War I there had been a large export trade from Dinorwic to foreign ports, Germany being the main market. The trade however was to sink to a low ebb after 1925 when only 13,864 tons were exported, 4940 tons of this going to Eire. By 1934 exports were barely 4566 tons (2202 to Eire), and so it went on. This drastic falling-off of export trade was due to the growing supply of cheaper slates and materials from elsewhere (which had already affected Penrhyn and the rest of the North Wales industry), coupled with a contraction of the Irish market due to the imposition in 1934 of a heavy tariff against imported slates. The table below clearly shows this decline in the shipment of slates (both coastwise and abroad) from Port Dinorwic.

| Year | Tons shipped | Year | Tons shipped |
| --- | --- | --- | --- |
| 1845 | 65,700 | 1895 | 65,000 |
| 1850 | 75,900 | 1900 | 61,700 |
| 1855 | 64,500 | 1905 | 64,200 |
| 1860 | 73,400 | 1910 | 56,600 |
| 1865 | 80,000 | 1915 | 27,500 |
| 1870 | 76,800 | 1920 | 19,300 |
| 1875 | 69,200 | 1925 | 33,500 |
| 1880 | 57,000 | 1930 | 9300 |
| 1885 | 45,200 | 1935 | 37,200 |
| 1890 | 55,900 | | |

## THE PORT DINORWIC INCLINE

The Port Dinorwic incline, known locally as the Rallt

incline, was constructed at the same time as the Padarn Railway in 1842-3. The railway had its terminus at Penscoins, above Port Dinorwic, and the incline ran from there down to the quay. (The upper terminus was also known as Carreg y Gwalch.) The double incline was ¼ mile long with a gradient of 1 in 4. Halfway down it crossed a minor road and then the Bangor-Caernarvon railway by wooden bridges, before entering a short cutting. It then passed beneath the Bangor-Caernarvon road (A487) in a short tunnel, levelling out at the lower tunnel mouth which was situated within the port itself.

The incline was originally worked using an endless chain. This ran down the centre of each track, passing round sheaves at the top and bottom. Loaded waggons were hooked on to the chain at the top and allowed to run down by gravity, pulling up the empty ones on the other track. This meant simply that one line of chain went up whilst the other side came down; unfortunately this also meant that not only did the loaded waggons have to raise the empty ones, they had in addition to draw around ½ mile of heavy steel chain in their wake. The chain ran over horizontal sheaves, set at intervals, down the centre of the two tracks; a slate footpath ran the length of the incline between the two lines. When the incline was in operation the loaded waggons descended in batches on the right hand track, looking down from above. Immediately outside the lower tunnel mouth was a small platform where a handful of men counted and checked the slates as the waggons emerged from the tunnel.

In the early years of the twentieth century, and especially after World War I, the traffic on the railway was noticeably lessening and hence there was less weight available to work the incline. This state of affairs led to the removal of the chain and sheaves in May 1924 and they were replaced by a more conventional system. This consisted of a steel cable round an overhead drum at the top of the incline. Constructed with the rest of the railway the incline, for the remainder of its life worked on the self-acting principle (as were those in the quarry), likewise closed along with the Padarn Railway and the port system on 27 October 1961.

Page 87:
(above) *Carefully posed late-nineteenth century scene at Gilfach Ddu showing both kinds of velocipedes and slate dressing operations;* (below) *fifty years on: a view from the A2 incline (at the top of the photo above) leading to the Mills section of the quarry. In the left distance is the Padarn's covered platform immediately below the hospital*

Page 88:
(above) *Loading the transporter wagons at Gilfach Ddu. Note the 2ft cast iron junction plates*; (below) *four-way wagon turntable preserved in situ in the Gilfach Ddu museum*

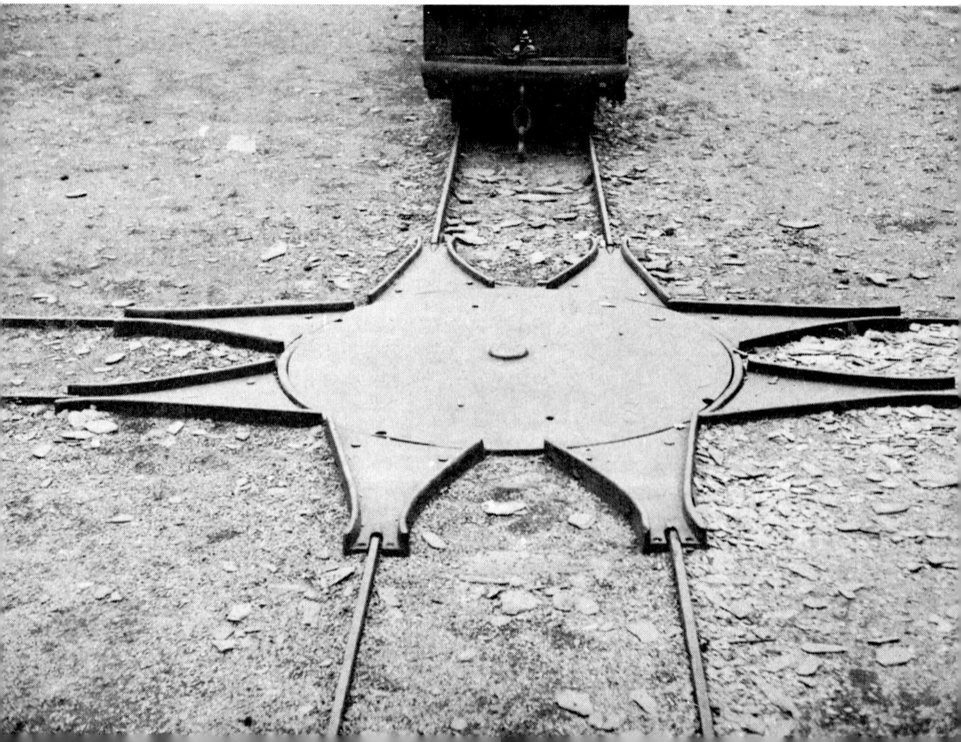

## THE PORT DINORWIC BRANCH

The line between Bangor and Caernarvon was promoted by an independent company, with Chester & Holyhead Railway support, and to that end the Bangor & Caernarvon Railway Act was passed on 20 May 1851. The company's main intention was to tap the Padarn Railway's slate traffic at Port Dinorwic and the line from the C & HR main line at Menai Bridge to Port Dinorwic was opened for slate traffic on 10 March 1852. The length of this branch was 3½ miles; the four mile extension to Caernarvon opened for passengers on 1 July of the same year and for freight shortly afterwards.

The single-track line travelled under the Port Dinorwic incline just above the upper tunnel mouth and transhipment of slates posed serious problems; problems that were solved in 1856 by the decision to construct a branch down to the actual port, roughly following the route of the final stretch of the old Dinorwic Tramroad. By March construction was well under way and later that summer the line reached the slate quay. As completed the single-track branch left the main B & C line (doubled 1872-4) at a point known as Port Siding, nearly one mile east of the village, and took a slightly divergent path to the west, dropping sharply down a ruling gradient of 1 in 42 through a cutting and under the Bangor-Caernarvon turnpike by means of a stone skew arch bridge. It was now in the small 'valley' of the stream which fed the dock at the port and continued to drop steadily to the quay. Here it doubled to form a transhipment siding and loop and skirted the landward edge of the port, crossed by the narrow gauge lines, to its termination, 1 mile 4 chains from its commencement.

The B & C was leased to the LNWR in 1859 and incorporated into that company eight years later; the C & HR had been similarly dealt with in 1858. The branch was controlled by the Port Siding signal box (strictly speaking the branch was not a branch but a siding with regard to its operation); here there was a large notice commanding engine drivers to stop their trains to pin down all brakes before venturing down the steep gradient. The last working to take place over the line was on 30 October 1961, just after the closure of the Padarn Railway. The track was lifted soon afterwards and the box removed. The road bridge still stands unaltered; above this the trackbed is, expectedly, densely overgrown with bushes and young trees; below the bridge the two hundred yards or so down to the port is, for the most part, used as an access road for lorries to storage tanks located beside the stream behind the port. The level stretch along the quayside is now being obliterated by landscaping and resurfacing. Gone too is the track from the main line, closed to passengers in 1970 and to goods in 1972.

WORKING

Both Port Penrhyn and Port Dinorwic were worked on much the same lines. Both were fed by their respective private railways; both later had added standard gauge transhipment sidings; both had one main slate quay and a harbour for waiting vessels; both operated their own fleet of slate ships. Other resemblances were such details as stables in the tramroad days, locomotive sheds in the railway days, stores, offices, weighhouses and all the general port paraphernalia.

When the slate arrived at the port, either in trainload via the Penrhyn Railway or in waggonload via the Port Dinorwic incline, the slates would first be checked and counted or weighed, then shunted in the waggons by one of the locomotives kept at the port for that purpose (see Chapters 5 and 7). Criss-crossing the slate quay was a network of waggon turntables and sidings running between the stacks of slates waiting for shipment; to these stacks would be added the new arrivals. When a particular ship was alongside the quay its cargo would be assembled, taken to the quayside and there transferred to the waiting vessels. This process was usually carried out either by sliding small batches of slates down wooden planks resting on the gunwale or by wheeling them in wheelbarrows up the planks, depending on the state of the tide.

The only real difference between the two ports was that Port Dinorwic was equipped with a dry dock, operated by a nominally independent company, the Port Dinorwic Dry Dock Co. Here vessels from all along the Menai Straits were repaired —and other work too was performed, such as repairs to the Snowdon Mountain Railway locomotives.

### LATER YEARS

By 1891 there were even fewer slate mines and quarries in North Wales than in 1885. The national railway system had proved a great blow to the slate fleets since it was now a means of cheaper conveyance to the furthest domestic markets, though as the Dinorwic slate was carried by rail from Port Dinorwic and not from the quarry the Padarn Railway remained unaffected by this new development. In 1895 in fact a third Hunslet 0-6-0 tank engine was bought for the railway. Identical to the earlier two, this was named *Velinheli*. But— despite national rail carriage it was fast becoming cheaper to import slates. In 1898 the number of men employed in the Dinorwic Quarry reached its high point of 3110 and British slate its maximum output of 634,000 tons, 488,000 tons of this being produced in North Wales.

As it entered the twentieth century the slate industry maintained this prosperous level for a while. In 1900 it was estimated that four out of every five houses were roofed with slates and there was a steady, if not remarkable, demand. In Caernarvonshire in 1909 the 99 existing quarries or mines employed 10,169 men (quarrying being the county's only industrial occupation), thus giving employment to a large number of hands in subsidiary industries and occupations. The county was in fact dangerously dependent upon the slate industry and now the tide was beginning to turn. The fact that four out of five houses were roofed with slates meant that the market was virtually saturated—further demand could only come from new houses and here Welsh slate faced increasing competition from imported slate and manufactured tiles. In 1911 the Dinorwic labour force had slipped to less than 2800 and in that year the quarry joined with Penrhyn to form an informal Quarry Proprietors' Association. This however proved ineffective and died away completely with the coming of World War I.

In 1917 the North Wales Slate Quarry Proprietors' Association was set up to represent all the local quarry employers but this too failed because the Dinorwic and Penrhyn Quarries jointly produced more slate than all the other thirty concerns put together and because there was a complete breakdown of all attempts at price fixing, especially when demand was slack. World War I had made the position of the quarries difficult: there had been a scarcity of skilled labour as many quarrymen were enlisted, never to return, and for the same reason recruitment of young men was hard. Soon the quarries were manned by old men and young boys; many others began to leave the slate areas to seek employment elsewhere. The labour force dropped to a third of that of the pre-war period and production fell drastically—extracting slate was predominantly a manual operation and there were just not the men to do it.

During the war, in Caernarvonshire alone, fourteen slate quarries and eleven mines closed, but trade picked up slightly in 1919 because of the backlog of repairs, rebuilding and reroofing. Between 1918 and 1920 the labour force in the *whole* of the North Wales industry increased from 3234 to 7937 and production rose from 101,000 to 190,000 tons. The boom broke in 1920 and this, and a winding-up of the Addison scheme of housing subsidies in July 1921, further retarded the industry's recovery. Added to this was the fact that Britain had lost much of its pre-war export trade with Germany, Austria, India, Australia, South Africa and the South American countries. In 1921 Dinorwic left the NWSQPA, mainly because it believed it was being undercut.

By the mid-1920s the slate industry was at a very low ebb. Flat-roofed houses, or houses with tiled roofs, were fashionable. It was no longer a case of Sir Francis Bacon's quote of 'Houses are built to live in and not to look on'. House buyers paid more attention to appearance than to durability: slate did not appeal. The *Caernarvon & Denbigh Herald* of 15

September 1922 noted that at Dinorwic 'the quarrymen commenced working five days this week. They had worked only four for several weeks. It is to be hoped that they will be working full-time before long'. Short time was in fact the order of the day throughout the industry for many years and the men were continually fighting to improve their low wages —wages far behind those of other industries, offering no inducement for young men to join the quarries. In May 1931 74 per cent of the insured workmen in the Llanberis district were temporarily unemployed because of the slump; for the whole year the figure was 20 per cent. (It dropped from 22 per cent in 1930 to 6 per cent in 1934 and remained near that level for some years.)

In 1937 Sir C. M. R. V. Duff-Assheton-Smith, the then owner of the Dinorwic Quarry, employed just 2369 men. By the following year barely one out of every five houses in Britain was now roofed with slate. The industry was at its lowest level ever. As soon as the blitz started, though, stocks were soon cleared but from 1940 onwards—just as had happened in World War I—the industry was left with a depleted and very ill-balanced labour force. In August 1940 Dinorwic was forced to close for nine weeks owing to the shortage of men. Three years later the only Caernarvonshire concern left in the NWSQPA was the Dorothea Slate Quarry Co Ltd of Nantlle, but in that same year the association revived to become fully representative once more. For a short time after the war there was an abnormally high demand as slate was needed for repairs.

The Dinorwic Quarry, worked since 1788, had yielded up its more productive and accessible slate beds while the proportion of rubble to good rock was increasing and hampering production. By 1946 the market was left wide open for other roofing materials because the quarries were finding it impossible to produce enough slates cheap enough to sell. Feet of useless rock covered the slate beds—waste that had to be removed manually as the industry was not one easily mechanised. The quarry needed to double its labour force to remain efficient but was unable to find the skilled men. The number employed was down to 1200 but even so unemployed men found it difficult to obtain work there as the management was reluctant to take on new hands: the policy was to reserve the better work places for its own ex-employees. It was eager to attract skilled quarrymen for the simple reason that it took six years to train a new worker. This was difficult however as the wages and conditions of work were well below other industries even though wages had risen appreciably from 8s per day in 1938 to 15s 2d in 1946. These wages, for skilled quarrymen, represented 44s and 83s 5d a week respectively. Taking into account risk of accident, the skilled nature of the work, arduous labour and unsatisfactory working conditions, the rate was not so favourable.

There was in fact room for great improvements in conditions in the quarry: better sheds and mills, appliances to eliminate slate dust (silica dust fatal to health), provision of works canteens, adequate drying facilities for wet clothes, mechanical devices to reduce the lifting of heavy weights and so on. The quarry company took steps to increase its young labour force but with no great success. A serious shortage of apprentices existed as the initial wage of 23s 4d a week was too low to attract them. Also, the quarrymen contractors were against a pay rise for apprentices since they had to pay the wages of trainees after the end of the first year. Even so, in 1946 the wages bill at Dinorwic amounted to 75 per cent of the total cost of production and the quarry was on the point of collapse.

### CLOSURE AND LIFTING

The post-war years were indeed bleak for the Dinorwic Quarry, and with it the Padarn Railway since the latter was totally dependent upon the former and accurately reflected its every change of fortune. New, lighter and cheaper materials were on the market and these were being used for repairing war damage. And so the demand for slate subsided. One by one the workers were forced to leave the quarry to seek employment less arduous and more remunerative, for the wages of a quarryman were pitiful compared to those of other workers.

The owners found they had to make men redundant in order to keep going. By 1958 the quarry was working part-time again and barely covering labour costs. By 1961 the slate train to the port was making a single daily journey at the most hauling seven or eight transporters—hardly remunerative operating—and it came as no surprise when the Padarn's closure was announced. The manager said that customers required their slates to be sent by road, although some might still be sent by rail from Llanberis (though this arrangement was to last only a year). A skeleton staff only was to be kept on at Port Dinorwic.

It was intended that the railway should close within two months of July 1961. In August a tender from Messrs Pittrail Ltd of Aldridge, Staffs, was accepted for the lifting and removal of the railway and its stock. The actual last working trip took place on 27 October from Gilfach Ddu to Penscoins and back, drawn by *Amalthaea* (the renamed *Pandora*). Within two years the Pittrail contract of £11,380 for the track and a further £3810 for the stock was completed. Between April and August 1963 the railway's three steam locomotives and one petrol locomotive, kept by Pittrail in the hope that some industrial concern might wish to purchase the complete stock, were scrapped. (Both the wish to dispose of the railway as a single lot and the lack of interest shown in such a proposition are accounted for quite simply by the railway's unusual gauge.) The track had already been lifted, working backwards from Penscoins using *Dinorwic* on the recovery train, between 16 May 1962 and February 1963.

MARCHLYN QUARRY

Marchlyn lies one mile northwards from Dinorwic, on the mountainside between the Dinorwic and the Penrhyn workings. A small attempt had been made in 1931 towards furthering the site as a slate quarry. This quarry, 1500ft above sea level, was worked on a small scale until 1958 when all quarrying operations were suspended. However, the old Dinorwic bed was coming to the end of its workable life and the quarry owners were looking for a new site to develop; eventually extensive core drilling tests led to proposed working on a large scale at Marchlyn using much-improved methods, modern equipment and road transport. Further investigations proved it to be a worthwhile venture and stripping operations began in June 1961. It was hoped that the quarry would be in production within three years and this in fact happened. The equipping of the quarry cost £100,000. Five galleries were planned, each 100yd long and 60ft high; at first the slate had to be sent to Dinorwic for dressing but this was later carried out on the site.

The move to Marchlyn had been a drastic step—a step that was to fail through no fault of its own. It met with unavoidable problems and unfavourable circumstances due to exterior economic factors and the difficulties facing the industry as a whole. There had been a steady drop in demand for slate, tiles being far more fashionable. Labour was difficult to find. Despite the setting-up of brick and tile works (both of Marsden design and sited on the level near the Muriau dressing shed) at Dinorwic to manufacture these products from slate granules obtained from waste rock, the quarry was steadily running down. In 1963 the company employed 700 men; in five years this was whittled down to exactly half that figure.

In July 1969 the last 350 quarry workers were laid off. In the *Guardian* of 21 August the company directors wrote their own obituary:

> Owing to the continuing decline for roofing slates, both in the home market and abroad, with a consequent heavy build-up of stocks, the directors have no alternative other than to recommend the appointment of a receiver by the debenture holders, one of whom is the Board of Trade.

### THE AUCTIONS

On Friday 12 and Saturday 13 December 1969 the Dinorwic Slate Quarries Co (as its title now was) sold by auction all its remaining Dinorwic and Port Dinorwic equipment, including four steam locomotives. The *Guardian* of 17 November 1969 referred to the forthcoming auction thus:

The machinery is at the century-old engineering workshops of Dinorwic slate quarry, Llanberis, Caernarvonshire, which closed in July soon after producing the dais used at Prince Charles' investiture. . . .
British and American preservation societies are expected to snap up the railways items which range from complete 2ft gauge locomotives to a hand-cranked velocipede truck.

Mr Henry Kenyon, of the Manchester firm of Rushton, Son & Kenyon arranging the auction, described the site as 'a gem of industrial archaeology'. The quarry and port machinery and stores were to be auctioned lock, stock and barrel.

On 13 December a Mr Alan Porter from Westcliff-on-Sea, Essex, spent a total of some £4000, most of it on three Hunslet steam locomotives: *Red Damsel* (£1550), *Dolbadarn* (£1050) and *Wild Aster* (£700); the rest went on spares and other equipment. The purpose of this expenditure was his plan for a passenger-carrying lakeside railway along the former Padarn Railway trackbed. (See Chapter 8 for the later history of this project.) At the same auction some of the antique machinery due to be sold to help pay off the company's debts was saved from the scrap heap by an order listing the quarry as an industrial monument with a view to turning the works at Gilfach Ddu into an industrial museum. Among the items so preserved was the de Winton 50ft water wheel; also saved was the quarry hospital, complete with amputation equipment and a stock of artificial eyes! (See Chapter 8.)

In May 1970 steps were taken to dispose of the quarry itself and on instructions from Mr. K. A. Millichap, the receiver and manager of the quarry, the Dinorwic and Marchlyn quarries were put up for auction. The press advertisements described the quarry as being 'the largest open slate quarry in the world with existing quarry workings extending to over 800 acres' and as having 'reserves of slate rock of over 1000 acres'. The annual production of roofing slates was given as 13,500 tons; the property included quarry offices, the manager's house, various other flats and tied properties and the fishing rights on Llyn Marchlyn Bach and Llyn Marchlyn Mawr. Also included in the property were woodlands, grazing enclosures and pastureland making 2000 acres in all. The public auction was held at the Royal Hotel, Caernarvon (the earlier auctions had been held at the quarry), on Tuesday, 23 June 1970. Particulars and plans were available from the auctioneers, John Pritchard & Co of Bangor.

The quarries themselves were sold for a paltry £19,000 to McAlpine & Sons 'after ten minutes of sluggish bidding that would have made the nineteenth-century quarryman weep in disbelief' (*Guardian* 24 June 1970). The winning bidder for and a

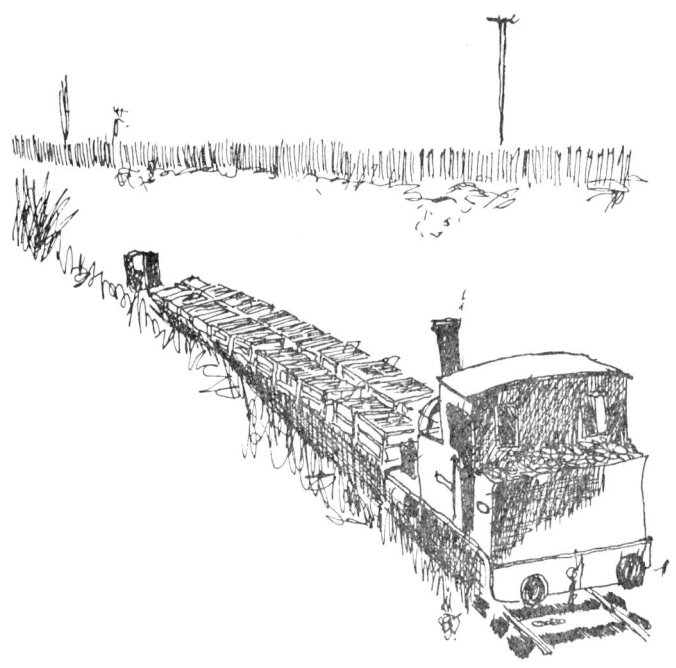

director of McAlpines, Mr P. H. Bell, said that the company's move was a 'holding operation' in case the market for slate improved or it became economically viable either to process the rock into another form or extract its mineral content (eg aluminium).

The workshops and undeveloped area were bought by the Caernarvonshire County Council; the modern slate processing machinery was sold the following day.

CHAPTER 5

# Penrhyn Stock

MAIN LINE LOCOMOTIVES

The nine locomotives which worked the Penrhyn Railway fall neatly into three groups of three. Each group was markedly different from the other two groups both in design and origin.

*The de Wintons*

The first three locomotives to work the main line when it opened were built by de Winton at the Union Foundry, Caernarvon. The name of this firm is usually associated with the small, vertical-boilered locomotives supplied to the North Wales slate and stone quarries (Dinorwic and Penrhyn amongst them); what set the three Penrhyn Railway locomotives apart was the fact that they were far more conventional in design, being 0-4-0 tank engines with normal horizontal boilers. Two inside cylinders drove on to a cranked axle. All three had outside frames. One, *Edward Sholto*, had a saddle tank while the other two, *Hilda* and *Violet*, had side tanks.

Following customary de Winton practice none of these locomotives had works numbers but it appears that *Edward Sholto* was the first to arrive at the quarry (by road) and began work on the section of the new line from the quarry to the top of the Dinas incline where the new route, still being constructed, diverged from the tramroad (1878). Then came *Hilda* and lastly *Violet* which was delivered by sea to Port Penrhyn, presumably in late 1878 or early 1879. Apart from this little is known about them. The last to arrive was the first to go for *Violet* was scrapped in 1902. *Edward Sholto* suffered likewise in 1907 and *Hilda* sometime after 1911.

*The Hunslets*

The first of these three locomotives was *Charles*, constructed in 1882 as works no 283 (order no 5950), code or class word Selra. It was somewhat similar in design to the early Hunslets at Dinorwic but altogether much larger and more powerful. It was an 0-4-0 saddle tank with outside cylinders and an overall cab. The cylinders were mounted above the buffer beam and sharply inclined to drive the rear axle. This design

was adopted in order to place the large (10in x 12in) cylinders within the loading gauge whilst at the same time enabling the crossheads to avoid fouling the cranks on the leading axle. The connecting rods were fitted behind the coupling rods, giving an overall impression of a very compact yet powerful machine. The wheels were 25in in diameter, set on a 5ft wheelbase. Weight in working order was $12\frac{1}{4}$ tons. After the closure of the line *Charles* was placed on permanent loan to the Museum of Industrial Locomotives at Penrhyn Castle in 1963.

In 1893 two more locomotives were built by Hunslet (order no 15420) to replace the less powerful de Wintons which were then transferred to quarry duties. The new Hunslets were almost identical to *Charles* except that they had 10½in diameter cylinders and enlarged fireboxes. They were named *Blanche* and *Linda* and carried works numbers 589 and 590 respectively. They survived the closure of the line along with *Charles* and were acquired by the Ffestiniog Railway, *Linda* in July 1962 and *Blanche* in December 1963.

*The Baldwins*
These last three locomotives to be used on the Penrhyn main line had been built at the Baldwin Locomotive Works, Philadelphia, USA, in 1917 as members of the 10/12/D5 class, works nos 46764, 46828 and 47143, and had been shipped to France for military use there on 2ft (60cm) gauge lines. Under the ownership of the United States Army Transportation Corps they were numbered USA5096, USA5104 and USA5159 respectively. In design they were identical 2-6-2 side tanks with 24in driving wheels on a coupled wheelbase of 6ft. The outside cylinders were 9in x 12in; boiler pressure was 175lb/sq in and the weight in working order 12 tons. After World War I many of these Baldwin military locomotives of differing designs found their way across to Britain (in Wales the Glyn Valley Tramway acquired a 4-6-0 side tank, as did the Welsh Highland Railway) and the three in question were purchased in 1923 for use on the Penrhyn Railway and regauged. For some reason they were numbered and named in reverse order to their works numbers as No 1 *Llandegai*, No 2 *Felin Hen* and No 3 *Tregarth*.

The Baldwins did not, however, prove to be as successful as was hoped for and within five years all three had been withdrawn, leaving the Hunslets to work the railway unaided. *Llandegai* was taken out of service in November 1927 and in March 1929 was stripped of all unnecessary parts for spares and used at its namesake village as a stationary boiler and engine to drive the estate sawmill. This duty was performed until July 1931 when the mill was moved; the remains of No 1 were thereupon removed to Port Penrhyn where they rested until being sold for scrap in January 1940. In that month a similar fate befell *Tregarth*, towed down to the port after lying at the quarry since its withdrawal in April 1928. No 2 *Felin Hen* escaped a similar fate for although withdrawn in June 1927 and stored at Port Penrhyn, it was put into working order again and sold in January 1940 to the Fairymead Sugar Milling Co of Bundaberg, Queensland, where it ran on the cane field railways, complete with spark arrester (and latterly as an 0-6-2T) until 1968 when it was retired and preserved, its global wanderings over.

### DE WINTONS

Besides the three main line locomotives the Union Foundry supplied a further seven engines to the Penrhyn Quarry. These were all 0-4-0 vertical-boilered tank engines with two vertical cylinders bolted to the front of the boiler. These drove the front cranked axle. Coupling rods transmitted the motion to the rear axle. The wheels were 20in in diameter and placed inside the frames on a 4ft 4in wheelbase. They represented the current de Winton design for quarry locomotives (they were similar to *Wellington* at Dinorwic) and were supplied in 1876-7.

*'Lord Penrhyn', 'Lady Penrhyn', 'Alice'*
These three were the first to be delivered, probably in 1876, and had 6in x 10in cylinders. They worked in the quarry until displaced by newer Hunslet locomotives (see later). *Lord Penrhyn* was scrapped in 1909 and the other two some time after 1911.

*'Georgina', 'Ina', 'Kathleen', 'George Henry'*
These four had larger 6in x 12in cylinders but were otherwise similar to the earlier three. The works plates of *Kathleen* and *George Henry* both survive and give construction dates of 1877. *Georgina* and *Ina* began work shunting at Port Penrhyn until 1883 when they were displaced by Hunslets. The de Wintons were then transferred to the quarry where they remained until withdrawal. *Georgina* was scrapped in 1904; the other three were withdrawn about 1911. *Ina* was then cut up and the other two stored. *Kathleen* was later dismantled

in 1939 but miraculously survived until January 1965 when it was acquired for private preservation. *George Henry* was sent to the Narrow Gauge Museum at Towyn for display in 1955.

### PORT CLASS

The three locomotives which made up this class were the next Hunslets to be purchased after *Charles*. They spent their life working primarily at Port Dinorwic—hence their name —and replaced the two de Wintons there. They had 7in x 10in cylinders and a 4ft wheelbase. They were generally similar to the rest of the Hunslets at both Penrhyn and Dinorwic, each class being designed for a particular requirement. In this case the Penrhyn Port class came midway in size between the Dinorwic Alice class and Mills class. Like the rest of the Hunslets they were 0-4-0 saddle tanks with outside cylinders. The boilers were domed; none are known to have carried cabs. Individually they were:

'Gwynedd'
Built in 1883 as works no 316, order no 6700, *Gwynedd* worked at the port until its closure. After being stored under cover it was acquired for preservation in 1964.

'Lillian'
Works no 317 of 1883, *Lillian* had a similar history to that of her sister engine before being sold for preservation in 1966; since 1958 she had lain derelict outside the quarry workshops.

'Winifred'
This was the last of the class and was constructed in 1885 as works no 364, order no 8020. In 1955 *Winifred* was replaced by a diesel locomotive and was transferred to the quarry where she worked on the top level, the William Parry gallery, until 1964. In 1965 she was shipped to the USA for preservation, leaving Manchester dock on board the *SS Manchester Progress* on 23 July.

### SMALL CLASS

This class of four locomotives was so-called because it was the smallest Hunslet design to work on the Penrhyn system; it was a design virtually identical to the Alice class at Dinorwic with the characteristic domeless boiler. All four engines worked exclusively in the quarry, originally supplementing the de Wintons there. As at Dinorwic, the design was an ideal one for use on light track with sharp curves and a restricted loading gauge.

*'Margaret'*
Works no 605 of 1894, order no 16350, *Margaret* was withdrawn in 1955 as unfit for service and was later acquired for preservation.

*'Alan George'*
Also built in 1894, this was works no 606 of the same order. It was purchased for preservation in August 1965.

*'Nesta'*
*Nesta* was works no 704 of 1899, constructed under order no 21900. She accompanied Port class *Winifred* to America in July 1965.

*'Elin'*
Sister engine to *Nesta*, this was works no 705 of 1899. She was acquired in July 1962 for preservation.

### LARGE CLASS

The last class of Hunslets to be supplied to work the quarry system was also the most powerful. Basically they were similar to the Port class locomotives but with a higher 140lb/sq in pressured boiler, an enlarged firebox and 7½in x 10in cylinders. They also lacked the dropped rear footplate of the Port class. They too never sported cabs.

Comparative dimensions of all the Penrhyn Hunslets are given in Appendix 9.

Page 105:
(above) Blanche *and Port Class* Winifred *shunting at Port Penrhyn. Note the sand bucket carried by the main line engine;* (below) *trackwork crossings at Port Penrhyn with slab wagons in the distance*

Page 106:
(above) Port Dinorwic incline in its chain-worked days. View is from the upper mouth of the tunnel to the port; just visible is the transfer shed at the top of the incline (Penscoins); (right) Dinorwic Port class No 1, running with long chimney; (below) Port Dinorwic: looking across LMS siding to Menai Straits. Track on left leads to the port incline. Note slate wheelbarrow and packing mallet on right

## 'Hugh Napier'

Works no 855 of 1904, order no 27240, this was the first of the new arrivals destined gradually to replace the de Wintons. By 1964 it was out of service and stored under cover in the quarry; in November 1966 it was transferred to the museum at Penrhyn Castle to join *Charles*.

## 'Pamela'

Constructed under order no 29450 in 1906 as works no 920, *Pamela* was withdrawn by 1961 with a faulty boiler. (This had been transferred ten years earlier from *Bronllwyd*—see below.) She was eventually purchased for preservation in October 1966.

## 'Sybil Mary'

Works no 921 of 1906, sister engine to *Pamela*, *Sybil Mary* was out of service and stored with *Hugh Napier* by 1964. In April 1966 she was sold for preservation.

## 'George Sholto'

Built in 1909 as works no 994, order no 31610, it was withdrawn and stored along with *Hugh Napier* and *Sybil Mary* before being sold for preservation in February 1966.

## 'Gertrude'

Constructed in 1909 as works no 995 and sister engine to the one above, she was the first of the class to be withdrawn and in September 1960 was shipped to Canada for display there.

## 'Edward Sholto'

This was the last of the class, works no 996 of 1909, the last of the trio of order no 31610 and the last new steam locomotive to be bought for the quarry. Along with *Gertrude* it was one of the first to go and by 1960 was laying derelict beside the quarry workshops. In October 1961 it was sold to a Canadian buyer and exported.

OTHERS

In addition to the ten de Wintons, three Baldwins and sixteen Hunslets already described, no less than fourteen other steam locomotives of a wide variety of type and manufacture have been employed in the quarry. The majority were purchased secondhand and apart from this the only other thing they have in common is the fact that they were all tank engines! Individual details of each locomotive are given below, in chronological order of their arrival at Penrhyn.

'Bronllwyd'

The history of this locomotive is shrouded in a great deal of mystery. It is believed to have been the locomotive named *Coetmor* which was used by Parry on the Penrhyn Railway construction contract in 1878. When the line was completed Parry apparently sold the engine to the quarry whereupon—for some unknown reason—it was renamed. In design it was an 0-4-0 vertical-boilered engine, believed to have been constructed by Hughes of the Valley Foundry, Holyhead. This firm is only known to have built one other similar locomotive, *Mona*, which worked in a quarry at Penmaenmawr. It could well be that *Mona* and *Coetmor* were actually one and the same; the latter possibly being a de Winton rebuild of the former—an unsatisfactory locomotive.

*Bronllwyd*, whatever its precise origins, soon proved to be equally unsatisfactory and was adapted as a stationary engine to drive a slate mill in the quarry. It was finally scrapped in 1906.

'George Sholto'

Even more mystery surrounds this engine! It was in use c1876 on the Penrhyn Tramroad, working the first section from the quarry to the top of the Cilgeraint incline. It was an 0-4-0 side tank locomotive with outside cylinders and carried the number 3 and a brass plate inscribed 'John Beatson, Derby, Contractor' as well as its name. This plate is believed to refer to its one-time owner, not its maker; it might have been another de Winton or a product of Henry Hughes' locomotive and tramway engine works at Loughborough. (This is possibly the same Hughes of the Valley Foundry, Holyhead!) In view of the location given on the engine plate, the latter alternative seems more likely; whatever its origin, it does not appear to have survived very long at Penrhyn.

'*Sgt Murphy*'

Constructed in 1918 by Kerr, Stuart & Co at the California Works, Stoke-on-Trent, *Sgt Murphy* was the first of twelve secondhand steam locomotives (apart from the Baldwins described earlier) to arrive at Penrhyn during the period 1922-31. It was originally designed as a member of the builders' Haig class of locomotives and was an 0-6-0 side tank developing a tractive effort of 4503lb at 85 per cent boiler pressure. Further dimensions were:

| | |
|---|---|
| Wheel diameter: | 2ft 0in |
| Wheelbase (total): | 4ft 7½in |
| Cylinders: | 8½in × 11in |
| Overall length: | 14ft 0in |
| Overall width: | 5ft 8¾in |
| Overall height: | 8ft 11in |
| Boiler presure: | 160lb/sq in |
| Weight in working order: | 10½ tons |

Originally used by the Admiralty at Benchly Dock, Monmouthshire, 3117 was purchased from A. H. Richards of Chepstow in 1922 and regauged at the quarry from 60cm to 1ft 10¾in. It was, by Penrhyn Quarry standards, large, heavy and somewhat unstable over the quarry lines. In an attempt to improve matters it was rebuilt in 1932 when the boiler and side tank assembly was lowered in the frames, giving the locomotive a squat and ugly appearance. It still retained its overall cab after the alterations. By 1960 it had been dumped alongside the quarry workshops and remained there until July 1964 when it was removed for preservation.

'*Lilla*'

This was the only Hunslet to be purchased secondhand for

the quarry and arrived from the Amalgamated Slate Association Ltd quarry at Cilgwyn in August 1928. Works no 554, order no 13760, it had been built in 1891 as a Lilla class locomotive. Its main specifications were:

| | |
|---|---|
| Wheel diameter: | 2ft 2in |
| Wheelbase: | 4ft 6in |
| Cylinders: | 8½in × 14in |
| Tank capacity: | 220gal |
| Fuel capacity: | 8½cu ft |
| Total heating surface: | 193sq ft |
| Grate area: | 3½sq ft |
| Weight empty: | 9¼ tons |
| Weight in working order: | 10¾ tons |

*Lilla* too had been dumped by 1960 and remained rusting away until purchased for preservation in December 1963.

'*Jubilee 1897*'

Built by Manning, Wardle at Leeds as works no 1382 in 1897, this was another ex-Cilgwyn locomotive. Also purchased in August 1928 it was regauged (along with *Lilla*) from 1ft 11½in at Bethesda. It was an 0-4-0 saddle tank with outside cylinders and frames and was fitted with an overall cab. Leading dimensions were:

| | |
|---|---|
| Wheel diameter: | 2ft 2in |
| Wheelbase: | 4ft 4in |
| Cylinders: | 9in × 14in |
| Boiler pressure: | 140lb/sq in |
| Weight in working order: | 11½ tons |

Dumped by 1960 as unfit for service, it was sent to the Narrow Gauge Museum at Towyn in December 1963.

'*Sanford*'

This locomotive was constructed for the Maenofferen Slate Quarry Co Ltd, Merioneth, by W. G. Bagnall at Stafford in 1900, works no 1571, and moved to Penrhyn in 1929. Leading dimensions of this 0-4-0 saddle tank were:

| | |
|---|---|
| Wheel diameter: | 1ft 8in |
| Wheelbase: | 3ft 0in |
| Cylinders: | 6in × 9in |
| Boiler pressure: | 140lb/sq in |
| Weight in working order: | 5 tons |

Weighing only five tons in running order, *Sanford* (and its sister engine *Skinner* described below) was the lightest locomotive to work in the quarry and was probably too underpowered to be of much use. It was out of service within ten years of its purchase and lay derelict until it was eventually converted into a ballast brake van, for details of which see the section below on the goods stock.

*'Skinner'*

Of a similar design to *Sanford*, this was Bagnall 1766 of 1906. It too came from Maenofferen Quarry in 1929 and was finally dismantled in 1954.

*'Eigiau'*

This locomotive was the sole example at the two major quarry systems of North Wales of the extremely productive Drewitz works of the Berlin firm of Orenstein & Koppel AG —perhaps in itself a fine tribute to the design of the Hunslets. It was constructed in 1912 as works no 5668 and was an 0-4-0 well tank with an overall cab. Its details were:

| | |
|---|---|
| Wheel diameter: | 1ft 7½in |
| Wheelbase: | 3ft 4in |
| Cylinders: | 6½in × 12in |
| Overall length: | 12ft 10in |
| Overall width: | 5ft 4in |
| Overall height: | 9ft 2in |
| Boiler pressure: | 175lb/sq in |
| Weight in working order: | 6½tons |
| Tractive effort at 85%: | 3868lb |

*Eigiau* was acquired in 1929 from the Aluminium Corporation works at Llyn Cowlyd Twy and regauged from 60cm. By 1960 it had been taken out of service and dumped beside the workshops; in February 1963 it was bought for preservation.

## 'Bronllwyd'

This 0-6-0 well tank originated at the Leeds works of Hudswell, Clarke & Co in 1930 as no 1643. It was delivered to Surrey County Council, numbered CP39, and used on 60cm gauge lines on various contracts. In December 1934 it was bought by Penrhyn Quarry and regauged; the backless cab was retained. *Bronllwyd* was not apparently named until 1937. Twelve years later it was withdrawn with a faulty boiler which was removed, repaired and used to replace that on *Pamela*. The remainder of the locomotive lay derelict until January 1966 when it was bought for preservation. Its principal dimensions were:

| | |
|---|---|
| Wheel diameter: | 1ft 11in |
| Wheelbase (total): | 4ft 2in |
| Cylinders: | 6½in × 12in |
| Boiler pressure: | 160lb/sq in |
| Weight in working order: | 6 tons 17cwt |

## 'Stanhope'

This was the second Kerr, Stuart locomotive to be bought for the quarry system and had originated in 1917 as works no 2395. It was a cabbed 0-4-2 saddle tank with principal dimensions:

| | |
|---|---|
| Wheel diameter (driving): | 2ft 0in |
| Wheel diameter (trailing): | 1ft 4½in |
| Wheelbase (coupled): | 3ft 0in |
| Wheelbase (total): | 7ft 6in |
| Cylinders: | 7in × 12in |
| Overall length: | 13ft 7in |
| Overall width: | 5ft 10¾in |
| Overall height: | 8ft 10in |
| Boiler pressure: | 160lb/sq in |
| Weight in working order: | 8½ tons |
| Tractive effort at 85%: | 3332lb |

*Stanhope* was the first of the builders' Tattoo class and was constructed for a Holloway Bros contract at Rosyth RN Dockyard in Scotland. In 1930 it passed into the hands of the Durham County Water Board for use on the Burhope Reservoir contract. Here it took its name from a nearby Weardale village. It was purchased in December 1934 by the Penrhyn Quarry and regauged from 60cm. After working for five years at Port Penrhyn it was transferred in 1940 to the quarry where it was withdrawn in 1947 and dumped beside the workshops. In 1953 many of its smaller components were sold to the Talyllyn Railway for use on a recently acquired Tattoo class engine *Edward Thomas* (ex-Corris Railway No 4). What remained continued to rust away until November 1966 when it was sold for its boiler which was subsequently used to repair *Bronllwyd* (see Chapter 8).

'Ogwen'

Built by the Avonside Engine Co of Bristol as works no 2066 in 1933, *Ogwen* was of the same design as *Elidir* at Dinorwic (see Chapter 7 for details). It was purchased from the Durham County Water Board in October 1936 after it had finished its work on the Burhope Reservoir construction; it followed *Stanhope* to Penrhyn where it acquired its name. It was still working at the beginning of 1964, only to be withdrawn shortly afterwards and shipped to America with *Winifred* in 1965.

'Marchlyn'

This was Avonside 2067 of 1933 and identical to *Ogwen*. It too came from Co Durham in October 1936 and lasted through to the end of steam at Penrhyn. It accompanied *Ogwen* across the Atlantic.

'Cegin'

Barclay 1991 of 1931, *Cegin* was built to the same design as No 70 at Dinorwic (see Chapter 7 for details) and was another ex-Durham County Water Board locomotive, purchased along with the two engines described above. It too lasted till the end of steam in the quarry and continued to stick to *Ogwen* and *Marchlyn* even after that when they travelled to the USA.

'*Glyder*'

The last of the secondhand steam locomotives, this was Barclay 1994 of 1931 and identical to *Cegin*. It was acquired from the same source at a slightly later date (January 1938) and after that followed an identical course to that of its sister engine.

### INTERNAL COMBUSTION

The pattern of events concerning the introduction of internal combustion locomotives at Penrhyn was surprisingly similar to that occurring at Dinorwic. The introduction was inevitable but again they did not succeed in replacing the steam locomotives. The first engine began work in the quarry in 1932; it was not until 1956 that one was used at Port Penrhyn and the Penrhyn Railway itself was exclusively steam worked to the last.

The Penrhyn internal combustion locomotives fall into two distinct groups. Between 1932 and 1939 a total of eighteen four-wheel petrol-mechanical locomotives were constructed in the Penrhyn workshops for use in the quarry. The power unit consisted of a Morris car engine. The locomotives were awarded the numbers 1-18. In May 1946 No 1 was rebuilt with a Lister diesel engine and proved so successful in its new form that a policy of buying secondhand diesel locomotives was instituted. By 1949 all the original petrol locomotives had been withdrawn with the exception of Nos 3, 8, 12, 15 and 16; these were all withdrawn shortly afterwards.

The second group of locomotives was comprised of those diesel locomotives purchased secondhand from a number of sources (either Ministry of Supply or various contractors) during the years 1946 to 1955. Twenty-two in all were purchased and were numbered 2-16 and 18-24. The rebuilt original No 1 retained its number in the new list; the new No 17 was an original frame fitted with a Ruston & Hornsby diesel engine —all the other locomotives were built by this firm at Lincoln. A complete stock list is given in Appendix 10.

The last locomotive to be purchased, No 24 in 1955, was put to work at Port Penrhyn; in the following years all the others worked solely at the quarry. With the closure of the rail system all were scrapped—with the exception of No 22 which was sold for preservation and No 24 which was sold to McAlpine & Son Ltd in January 1967 for use on the construction of the Deanhead Reservoir in Yorkshire. Later that year it too was acquired for private preservation.

PASSENGER STOCK

The Penrhyn passenger stock fleet was made up of quarrymen's carriages, a special saloon and a number of incline carriages.

*Quarrymen's carriages*

These were very simple and austere vehicles, running on four 15½in wheels; the wheelbase was 5ft 6in. In all sixteen were constructed between 1878 and 1908; the first batch were believed to have been de Winton products, the second to have been constructed at Penrhyn during the years 1904-8. The wooden bodywork lacked both roof and doors: no weather protection at all was provided and three openings in either side gave access to the six cross benches. Seating was for twenty-four workmen—at a pinch! A simple hook coupling was fitted at each end; the brake lever projected vertically above the side. Each carriage was lettered in the series A-P.

After the termination of the workmen's special trains in 1951 the vehicles were superfluous to the quarry's needs but seven escaped immediate scrapping. In 1952 H and P were donated to the Talyllyn Railway after regauging and the fitting of springs had taken place at Penrhyn; these became TR Nos 7 and 8. No 7 was also fitted with a light roof. 1953-4 C, D, E and G were purchased by the TR: E and G were cannibalised for spares for Nos 7 and 8 and for parts to be incorporated into No 10. C and D were combined as a bogie vehicle, No 9. As a result of a succession of rebuilds and replacements none of the Penrhyn bodies now survive.

The seventh carriage to escape scrapping is now preserved at Penrhyn Castle. Though now unlettered, it still retains its wooden brake blocks (operating on one axle) and compartment numbers.

*Incline carriages*

The quarry operated an unknown number of four-wheeled wooden incline carriages with high-sided wooden bodies. Seating was for six on three forward-facing seats. They were used, like those at Dinorwic, for conveying visitors around the quarry and up and down the inclines; one survives in the Penrhyn Castle museum. They were fitted with standard hook and link couplings and single-flanged wheels.

*Lord Penrhyn's Saloon*

This vehicle was built for the sole use of Lord Penrhyn, his family, guests and agent in 1882 at the quarry works. It was fitted with four 20in wheels on a 5ft wheelbase. It was a closed carriage with full glazing and curtains and held twenty passengers in slightly crowded comfort on its navy blue upholstery. It too was donated to the museum at Penrhyn Castle in 1963.

Overall body length of this vehicle is 11ft 10in; width 5ft 6in and height 8ft 0in. Livery is navy blue with white panels, lined out in gold and red. A small crest appears on the end door on either side.

GOODS STOCK

*Penrhyn Railway*

The bulk of the main line stock was made up of slate waggons for transporting the finished product. These were small four-wheeled trucks running on $15\frac{1}{2}$in wheels on a 2ft 10in wheelbase. In appearance they were somewhat different from those used at Dinorwic and in fact represented the other main type of slate waggon used in North Wales by having open sides formed from flat strips of metal, not rods and spacers. Each was roughly 6ft long, 3ft wide and 3ft 2in high, holding about two tons of slate. Weight empty was 12cwt. There were 390 of these slate waggons in use on the Penrhyn Railway altogether though accidents and repairs cut down the actual number running from one day to the next.

In addition there were ninety similar sized Fullersite waggons with timber sides, tare weight 6½cwt, used for carrying bags of Fullersite (powdered slate) down to the port; seventy flat bolsters for carrying slate slabs (or in pairs for timber and other long loads) and fifty wooden coal trucks (tare weight 9½cwt). The final vehicle used on the main line was a unique van constructed in 1956 from the remains of *Sanford*. On the engine frames was mounted a large water tank (as ballast to supply the necessary braking power) and a wooden cab, complete with look-out windows, for the brakesman. A screw handle operated the brake.

All rolling stock used on the main line was fitted with combined centre buffers, coupling hooks and single-flanged wheels.

*Quarry*

For working in the quarry complex a wide variety of waggons was used for transporting slate blocks and slabs, rough slates, waste rock and machinery. Basically they were simple four-wheeled vehicles built with the minimum of refinements. All were fitted with $15\frac{1}{2}$in diameter wheels, double-flanged and loose on their axles for working the rough tracks up to the workfaces. Like the main line stock, all were equipped with combined centre buffers and hook and link couplings. They numbered over 2000 in the heyday of the quarry.

CHAPTER 6

# *Padarn Stock and Working*

### WORKMEN'S TRANSPORT

The first form of transport used on the Padarn Railway, unique among the North Wales slate railways, was the velocipede: a large-wheeled truck propelled either by foot or hand power. A procession of these vehicles would journey to the quarry in the morning and back at night, officially in an orderly manner. It was, however, in practice a dangerous method of conveyance since different gangs of men would race each other along the line at speeds up to 40mph or so; if a man lost control of his crank handle at speed accidents could—and did—result. Despite this, velocipedes lasted on the railway for over forty years, from the opening of the new line in 1843, or more likely shortly afterwards (certainly by 1850), until 1895. Each was owned and used by a syndicate of men though 'outsiders' could occupy vacant seats at a charge of 6d a week. Further details of the construction of these machines are given later in the chapter.

By 1890 the labour force of the Dinorwic Quarry came from as far away as Port Dinorwic or even Anglesey; it was no longer restricted to the near-lying villages of Dinorwic, Deiniolen, Cwmglas, Llanberis, Penisarwaen, Fachwen and so forth —hence the use of velocipedes. The quarrymen in the main travelled daily to and from the quarry but those who came from further afield lived in barracks at the quarry and returned home only at weekends. At Penrhyn Quarry a special quarrymen's train was in use; this idea had once been under the consideration of the Dinorwic Quarry management but had been abandoned because of certain difficulties—mainly reluctance on the part of the general manager to finance a similar scheme. In 1892, dissatisfied with the velocipedes, the quarrymen themselves revived the issue.

On 15 September 1892 Isaac Parry and Hugh Griffith, acting as representatives of the Bethel quarrymen, wrote to the Hon W. W. Vivian, the quarry manager, that

> Among Mr Assheton-Smith's employees living at Bethel there has for a considerable time existed a strongly felt desire for some mode of conveyance to and from the quarries.

Two 'numerously attended meetings' held at Bethel Board School had resulted in this matter being laid before their employers. Vivian's reply was discouraging. He wrote that he considered their letter vague and asked them to be precise as to the actual concessions sought. The men were forced to make definite suggestions, chiefly based on the Penrhyn scheme, and on 19 September wrote asking whether it would be feasible for the workmen to be conveyed to and from work by means of the Padarn locomotives (and presumably the transporter waggons). They asked if Assheton-Smith would be prepared to entertain such a project and, if so, what terms would have to be considered. Again the response from Vivian was a cool one and he referred back to the numerous obstacles that had presented themselves when the matter had been previously contemplated. But there was a faint glimmer of hope when he invited the men to expand their proposals and promised to forward their request to Assheton-Smith—although his letter to the quarry owner put the matter in a very unfavourable light:

> So far as I can see there is but a bare possibility of one small benefit arising therefrom, against considerable extra costs for coals and oil, together with considerable wear and tear for the engine, about 30 main line trucks and about 120 small trucks, together with considerable wear and tear on the main line.

Vivian continued to point out the liability Assheton-Smith might incur for accidents and the fact that he feared people from Llanberis would migrate to Bethel, Llanrug and Capel Seion, bringing a deficiency of tenants to the Vaynol estate and subsequent loss of rents. Assheton-Smith however was more ready to agree to listen to the proposed scheme and did not foresee the calamities his manager saw. He did refuse, though, finally for fear of being held responsible for any accidents:

> I decline to risk taking passengers by a train not meant for that purpose unless I am exonerated from all risk in case of any accident taking place.

Undaunted, the quarrymen developed their argument. Their letter of 28 September asked if Assheton-Smith had legal powers to convey his men to work in return for payment. As an alternative, they suggested that he might build special carriages and charge the workmen a rate of interest on the capital invested, whilst retaining a few of the velocipedes for employees working irregular hours. The men went so far as to offer to construct the carriages themselves were he to lend them the required money. Their keenness, the offer to pay for the service and their long-term plans impressed Assheton-Smith but still he was concerned to avoid liability for accidents. He therefore agreed to the scheme on condition that the users of the train should sign an agreement to this effect and expressly stated that the institution of a quarrymen's train service was done as a favour and was 'a privilege entirely for the benefit and convenience of the employees'.

The management was sufficiently convinced to spend some capital on the project. Enquiries were made as to the possibility of purchasing purpose-built carriages. Meanwhile there were still many minor difficulties and questions such as: Do sick men continue to pay travelling fees? What of those who travel once a week if they decide to go more often? Where will the train stop? Were there to be arrangements for men to be in the same carriage and same seat each day to avoid a

# NOTICE.

## DINORWIC QUARRY RAILWAY.

For the convenience of Employees residing at a distance from the Quarries on the route of the Padarn Railway, permission will be given to travel on such Railway on the following terms and conditions :—

The use of such Railway is not to be considered as forming any part of the contract of employment, but is a privilege granted entirely for the benefit and convenience of the Employees ; and in consideration of such privilege all persons permitted to use such Railway agree and undertake to release and indemnify the owner from all claims and demands arising out of, or in respect of any accident or injury sustained by him or them whilst so using the same.

Such permission can be given or with-held at the sole discretion of the General Manager and may at any time and for any reason be revoked by him.

The Owner and Management shall not be responsible for any accident or injury occuring to any person permitted to use the Railway from any cause whatever and the use of such Railway shall at all times be at the sole risk of the Employee.

With a view of avoiding accidents Employees are required to observe the following regulations :—

No Velocipede, truck, carriage or conveyance shall be put upon or used on the Railway without the written permit (Caniatad) of the General Manager.

Employees shall not get into, or out of any such velocipede wagon or other conveyance whilst in motion, and such velocipede or other conveyance shall not travel at such a rate of speed as to endanger the persons riding in them, or any other person travelling on the Railway.

A distance of at least 25 yards shall be maintained between each Velocipede or other conveyance whilst travelling.

No Velocipede or other conveyance shall travel on the Railway whilst a train or engine is on the road without a written permit (Caniatad) from the Local Manager.

When permitted to travel by Quarry train all Employees must observe the orders and directions of the Guard or other person in charge of the train.

They must not attempt to enter or leave the train whilst the same is in motion.

They must not overcrowd the wagons or trucks and they must not attempt to ride on the engine.

**W. W. VIVIAN,**
Director and General Manager.

Dinorwic Quarry Office
April 3rd, 1894.

Page 123:
(above) Blanche *on returning workmen's train in the last years of the Penrhyn service. At the far end of the yard is the incline up to the main Office level of the quarry;* (below) *the halfway passing loop on the Penrhyn, seen from the rear of the quarry-bound train*

Page 124:
(above) *Coed y Parc looking towards the Penrhyn Quarry. Main line on the right, engine and general repair works over to the left;* (below) *Port Penrhyn engine shed, 1973. The carriage shed is on the left*

rush and overcrowding? What was the best way of disposing of the velocipedes? These were all eventually resolved and an amicable agreement reached though the quarry manager was empowered to revoke permission to use the train in individual cases. Arrangements continued throughout 1893 and 1894; on 18 December of that latter year it was decided by the management that notices would be erected near the points where the train would stop, stating that all persons entering the premises or travelling on the trains without having signed the agreement deposited at the quarry office would be treated as trespassers. These 'premises' were at Penscoins, Bethel, Pontrhythallt, Craig Dinas (Stabla) and Penllyn. At these points platforms were erected; a platform and awning was constructed at Gilfach Ddu and a carriage shed at Bethel. On 23 February 1895 the following table was drawn up to show the workmen to be picked up:

| Penscoins | Bethel | Pontrhythallt | Stabla | Penllyn | Total |
|-----------|--------|---------------|--------|---------|-------|
| 196       | 184    | 420           | 101    | 230     | 1,131 |

At this time the Gloucester Railway Carriage & Waggon Co was asked by the Dinorwic company to submit a design for an open workmen's carriage. This was done and the design agreed to with the provision that the carriages should be closed (hence the impression given by the finished carriages that the upper bodywork was designed and added on afterwards). New specifications were drawn up and an order placed for thirteen ordinary carriages at £118 each and four brake carriages at £127 each. There then ensued a certain amount of wrangling and discussion as to the various discounts that could be offered; the contract finally decided upon on 4 March 1895 was for fifteen ordinary carriages at £105 6s and four brake carriages at £113, making a total of £2031 10s—though this order was then increased by four ordinary carriages.

Certain rules and regulations that had to be met with were laid down: the carriage foreman would be dismissed if other than workmen were found on the train; employees were to travel in a numbered seat and carriage (the latter was actually

## DINORWIC QUARRIES RAILWAY.

Name of person..........................................

Address..........................................

Date issued........................By whom........................

The user of this ticket travels entirely at his or her own risk.

*(see other side)*

O. T. WILLIAMS,
General Manager.

---

ALL persons permitted to use the Padarn Railway agree and undertake to release and indemnify the owner from all claims and demands arising out of, or in respect of any accident or injury sustained by him or them whilst so using the same. The Owner and Management shall not be responsible for any accident or injury occuring to any person permitted to use the Railway from any cause whatever, and the use of such Railway shall at all times be at the sole risk of the person holding this ticket. When permitted to travel by Quarry train all persons must observe the orders and directions of the Guard or other person in charge of the train. They must not attempt to enter or leave the train whilst the same is in motion.

Oa 3/33

O. T. WILLIAMS,
General Manager.

*Padarn Railway workman's ticket, both sides*

---

## DINORWIC QUARRIES WORKMEN'S TRAIN.

This train leaves PENSCOINS each morning One hour and thirty minutes before the first Quarry Whistle.

Same leaves CEFN GWYN Crossing  5 min. after leaving Penscoins.
„         BETHEL         -  13  „
„         PENSARN        -  18  „
„         PONTRHYTHALLT  .  27  „
„         PENLLYN        .  33  „
Arriving at DINORWIC QUARRIES 44.  „

The train leaves the DINORWIC QUARRIES each day (except Saturdays) 30 minutes after the last Quarry Whistle.

On SATURDAYS 35 minutes after the last Quarry Whistle.

(Signed) W. W. VIVIAN,
Director & General Manager.

Dinorwic Quarry Office,
December 1st, 1896.

lettered, not numbered) and these were allotted to him by ticket; the employees were to comply with orders re shunting and were not allowed to move while the train was in motion. On the Tuesday following payday (monthly Fridays) the workmen had to pay the foreman of the carriage in which they travelled their monthly contributions to expenses. The foreman was also held responsible for any damage to windows, doors and number plates. Any workman suffering from infectious disease or using offensive language was to be immediately ejected! The journey from end to end of the railway was timed at forty-four minutes. The men's scale of contributions was:

| | |
|---|---|
| Penscoins | 2s 6d |
| Bethel | 2s 3d |
| Stabla; Pontrhythallt | 1s 10d |
| Penllyn | 1s 3d |

The commencement of the official workmen's train service in 1895 (the exact date is not recorded) spelt the end of the velocipedes on the Padarn Railway. Most of these unique machines were scrapped though a handful were maintained as useful permanent way inspection trolleys. Also at an end was the men's practice of riding on the slate trains; it may have been assumed from the above that this practice was not permitted. It was in actual fact as this notice of 11 February 1892 shows:

TILL FURTHER NOTICE EACH MONDAY MORNING THE FIRST TRAIN LEAVING "THE PORT END" WILL STOP TO PICK UP PERSONS EMPLOYED IN THE DINORWIC QUARRIES AT BETHEL AND PONTRHYTHALLT.

THE LAST TRAIN LEAVING THE QUARRIES ON SATURDAYS AND PAY DAYS WILL STOP TO DROP MEN AT PONTRHYTHALLT AND BETHEL.

ALL PERSONS TRAVELLING ON THIS LINE DO SO AT THEIR OWN RISK.

W. W. VIVIAN

This was presumably for the benefit of the workmen who lodged at the quarry during the week and returned home for the weekend.

The quarrymen's train service ceased on 8 November 1947. It was by then down to a mere three coaches.

### WORKING

The pattern of conveying slates was relatively simple. At the quarry the slates were loaded into quarry waggons; these waggons were in turn loaded on to transporters on the Padarn Railway at Gilfach Ddu. Each transporter carried four waggons, except the last of the train which held three and a narrow gauge guard's van. The transporters were locked into the loading dock while the slate waggons were either loaded on or off them. During transit the slate waggons were locked on to their transporters.

The train of transporter waggons was then taken by one of the Padarn locomotives, running cab first, to Penscoins. Here the narrow gauge waggons were let down the incline to the port, the transporters remaining at the top. The returning empty waggons were then loaded on to the empty transporters and taken back to the quarry where they were examined in a tumbler before being allowed up the quarry inclines.

At the end of the nineteenth century the line was being worked on a train staff system; it was the train crews' duty each day to sign the Staff System Book:

> We clearly understand that when two of the Main Line Engines are ordered to be worked, or are working, that we ie, two Engine Drivers, two Stokers, & two Guards are to work same upon the Main Line, on a Staff System, that is to say, the Engine which takes the Run down to the Port is to wait at Port without moving until arrival of the Workmens Train with Engine. And the Driver of the Workmens train is to hand the Staff to Driver of the Engine waiting with Run. We clearly understand that any infringement of these instructions, we are to be instantaneously dismissed, & that we forfeit all wages due. It is the duty of each of us to

## PADARN STOCK AND WORKING

sign "Staff System Book" prior to departure of either Engine. Later additional rules and regulations were imposed:

> The Engine Driver is to blow the whistle of his Engine in the Cutting before the embankment before the level crossing, the Quarry side of Bethel going down. In coming back the whistle is to be blown from the small footbridge over the line until the level crossing is reached.
> 
> (11 May 1897)
>
> No person is allowed to travel on the Engine on Padarn Railway Tramline, without permission, and no person is allowed to drive same without a written permission.
>
> (7 April 1897)
>
> All Flagmen must be at their respective Railway Crossings five minutes before the Workmen's Train is due to pass in the morning, and they must remain at their posts until Workmen's Train has passed in the evening.
>
> On approach of any Quarry Train to Level Crossings the Flagman must close the gates to all Road Traffic until the Quarry Train has cleared his crossing, then he is to immediately open his Road gates. Flagmen are to keep their telephone huts in a thoroughly clean condition, and should anything unusual happen on the line, they are to immediately telephone to the Quarry Office at Gilfach Ddu and Port Dinorwic.
>
> (6 May 1926)

The above rule was a direct result of the fatal 1926 accident (see below), as was the rule quoted below signed by the train crew involved:

> You are to bring your train when approaching Level Crossings at a speed to enable you to stop in two yards.
>
> Our signature signifies that this rule has been made clear to us.

The crossing gates at each level crossing had to be unlocked five minutes before the workmen's train arrived; they were relocked after it passed in the evening. All the crossings and both the termini were protected by semaphore signals on tall lattice masts. The crossing keepers were advised of an approach-

## INSTRUCTIONS TO ALL PADARN RAILWAY FLAGMEN

All Flagmen must be at their respective Railway Crossings five minutes before the Workmen's Train is due to pass in the morning, and they must remain at their posts until the Workmen's Train has passed in the evening.

On the approach of any Quarry Train to Level Crossings the Flagman must close the gates to all Road Traffic until the Quarry Train has cleared his Crossing, then he is to immediately open his Road gates.

Flagmen are to keep their telephone huts in a thoroughly clean condition, and should anything unusual happen on the line, they are to immediately telephone to the Quarry Office at Gilfach Ddu and Port Dinorwic.

Dinorwic Quarry Office
May 6th 1927

---

## CYFARWYDDIADAU I FLAGMEN PADARN RAILWAY

Rhaid i'r Flagmen fod gyda'u gwaith pum munud cyn amser penodedig i dren y gweithwyr fyned heibio yn y boreu, a rhaid iddynt aros wrth eu gwaith hyd nes y bydd tren y gweithwyr wedi myned heibio yn yr hwyr.

Ar ddyfodiad tren y Chwarel tuag at y Groesffordd, rhaid i'r Flagmen gau y llidiart yn erbyn pob trafnidiaeth arall, hyd nes y bydd tren y Chwarel wedi clirio, wedi hynny agorer y llidiart ar unwaith.

Y mae y Flagmen i gadw ystafell y telephone mewn cyflwr hollol lan, ac os digwydd unrhyw beth anghyffredin ar y reilffordd y maent i telephonio ar unwaith i Swyddfa Gilfach Ddu, a Porth Dinorwig.

Swyddfa Chwarel Dinorwig,
Mai 6ed 1927.

ing train by telephone. By the time of World War I the line was being worked on the one engine in steam principle, due to the fall in traffic, leaving one as a stand-by and one under repair at any one time.

### ACCIDENTS

On 7 April 1899, at about 12.30 pm, Henry Parry of Llanddeiniolen, a carter and tenant of Assheton-Smith, was involved in an accident with a train at Bethel level crossing. The incident was witnessed by several people: Hugh Jones, a blacksmith of Llangybi; Elias Jones, a carpenter of Porthmadog; a tailor and postman, Thomas Henry Williams; and two girls. They all said that the train was travelling at 'an extraordinary speed' (thus breaking the regulation 10mph limit) and was unable to pull up even though the driver could almost certainly have foreseen the accident. The engine whistle was not blown until too near the crossing—again breaking the railway's rules. The carter was unable to back his horse and cart off the crossing because of the steepness of the road at that point and his unwieldy load; he was forced to proceed. Thomas Williams, whose shop was close by the crossing, banged on his window to draw the carter's attention to the oncoming train, but Parry thought that he was trying to tell him that his load was loose. Williams confirmed the fact that the engine (approaching from the quarry) was at the Bethel end of the station platform, just 185ft from the road, before he heard the whistle. The damage to the engine caused by the collision amounted to £7 10s and the repairs to the wall cost £1. Parry's damages were far greater. He claimed £50 for the loss of his mare, £14 for the cart and £4 for the harness, making a total of £68. As the claim was for over £50 a High Court action could be brought for the damages; as Assheton-Smith's solicitor pointed out, the evidence of so many independent witnesses would carry far more weight than that of company employees (ie the train crew) and so the matter was settled out of court, Parry receiving £60. The rule of sounding the engine whistle on approaching a crossing was henceforth more rigorously enforced.

Despite these stricter measures accidents continued to be caused in this fashion. Less than a year later, on 17 January 1900, a Mr Pritchard received the sum of £32 10s for the loss of a horse and damage to a trap as a result of an accident. This had occurred at the Penllyn level crossing when a quarry train had collided with Pritchard's horse and trap; the vehicle had been driven at the time by a servant. The weight of the engine and its load came to over 100 tons and there was little chance of its being pulled up within a short distance, even though the trap had been seen on the line. Pritchard's original claim had been for £25 as the value of the mare, £8 for the loss of the trap, £4 for the harness, loss of wages for himself and his man £3 10s, and for burying the remains £1. 'Consequential damages' were also claimed, amounting to £5, thereby making an overall total of £46 10s. It was decided however that no consequential damages or loss of wages should be paid and £5 10s was deducted from the value of the mare, making a new total of £32 10s. This was agreed to by Mr Pritchard and subsequently paid.

There is still one serious accident on the Padarn Railway to consider. It involved a quarry train and an oil lorry. The inquest on the two occupants of the oil lorry was held on Saturday 23 January 1926; the fatal accident had occurred the previous day. The *Caernarvon & Denbigh Herald* recorded the facts the following week. The inquest was held at the YMCA, Bethel, by Mr J. Pentir Williams, the coroner for north Caernarvonshire, on the bodies of Thomas Williams, 48 years of age, of New Street, Caernarvon, and his mate William David Williams, 19 years of age, of Victoria Street, Caernarvon. Both had died the previous morning when a quarry train from Gilfach Ddu, fully loaded with slate, had dashed into the oil lorry on the Bethel level crossing.

Isaac Williams, of Tyddyn Andrew Isaf, Bethel, was the chief witness. He claimed that he had been standing at the hay shed near the level crossing, at 11.30 am, when he saw the train approaching. The engine was whistling, as was customary, until it reached the crossing. He saw the motor lorry going up the road near the church at Saron; it was travelling very slowly towards the crossing but did not stop. The engine ploughed into the lorry; Mr Williams, being about 250yd away, heard the impact and saw 'a great flame'.

The lorry was travelling from Bethel along the main road and so there was no doubt that the driver had had a clear view of the railway. The lorry often travelled this way and the driver was familiar with the route. The witness remembered (he had lived at Tyddyn Andrew Isaf for thirty years) a horse being killed there at the turn of the century—the 1899 accident.

The second witness called was William Evans, of Penrallt Cottages, Port Dinorwic, the driver of the slate train. He had been employed by the company for twenty-six years and, as was very probable, claimed to know every foot of the line. He stated that the train had started from the quarry on the Friday morning at 10.55 am. It had stopped near the Crauria Slate Works for about four minutes and eventually reached the level crossing at approximately 11.30 am. It was customary for the driver to shut off steam when going down a gradient and the speed of the engine had consistently been 10mph. The driver blew the whistle on approaching the crossing; he had seen the oil lorry 60yd away near the church when the train passed the carriage shed at Bethel.

Evans stated that the lorry stopped on reaching the crossing and then restarted in an attempt to cross the line in front of the train. On seeing this Evans applied the brakes and put the engine into reverse—but alas it was too late: the lorry had been struck by the engine and partly crushed against a slate wall. The rest of the lorry went under the engine.

PC Nicholas was then called and, replying to the coroner, said that he was at the scene of the accident at 11.40 am and saw the two men under the train. The train consisted of twenty-two trucks, fully laden, making it impossible for the train to pull up sharp in a distance of even 50yd from a speed of 10mph. There was no indication as to when the brakes had been applied as the rails had been wet. The constable agreed that the railway was on a higher level than the main road and consequently it was easier to see anything on the road from the railway than vice versa. There was no man at the crossing to give warning of an approaching train and no warning notice. About 80ft of wall had been demolished on the left hand side of the line; the lorry had been taken 84ft by the collision. He further stated that there were no protective gates on the crossing which could be closed against road traffic although gates on the railway itself were closed at night.

Owen John Roberts, of Sea View Terrace, Port Dinorwic, was the guard on duty. In his account he too stated that the train had departed at 10.55 am and had stopped at Mr T. R. Jones' mill (Crauria) before arriving at the crossing at 11.30 am. He agreed with the driver on all details but as he was at the far end of the train he had heard no sound of the impact. He said that the driver was careful but admitted that the train could not have been successfully halted in so short a distance. The fireman, Thomas Evans of Bridge Street, Port Dinorwic, corroborated all the evidence.

Dr Gwilym ap Vychan Jones was then called as a witness. He was in Bethel when PC Nicholas informed him of the terrible accident at the crossing and had accompanied the policeman to the scene where they found the bodies of the two men. One was under one of the waggons, still warm but dead from a fractured skull, with the right arm amputated at the elbow. This proved to be the body of Thomas Williams. The boy was under the engine with a smashed skull. Both men had suffered superficial burns but death must have been instantaneous. The bodies were removed to the YMCA hut.

The coroner drew the inquest to a conclusion. He decided that all involved were capable men and blame could be attached to no-one. The lorry driver had stopped, changed his mind and proceeded—if he had travelled just slightly faster he would have cleared the crossing. The lorry had been in perfect running order. He was also aware that over the past six months there had been several complaints that the crossing was a death trap. The jury went to discuss their verdict and returned twenty minutes later with a verdict of accidental death—indeed no other verdict could have been drawn. They did however make the following suggestions:

PADARN STOCK AND WORKING 135

1: Gates were to be placed at the crossing and until this was done a flagman was to be stationed there.
2: A heavier brake was to be attached to the train.
3: All crossings along the line were to be similarly protected.
4: The county council should put up notices at the crossings warning people of the danger.

### LOCOMOTIVES

The total number of locomotives which worked over the Padarn Railway metals was six: five were steam and one petrol. The five steam engines divide neatly in terms of age and design into two separate and quite distinct classes for which a table of comparative dimensions can be found in Appendix 3.

*The Horlocks*
To work the newly-constructed railway two locomotives were ordered from the Kent firm of A. Horlock & Co, marine and general engineers of the Northfleet Iron Works, Kent. The likely assumption is that the firm had supplied machinery to the quarry and port before and were therefore asked to supply the two locomotives as well. (A very similar state of affairs existed some quarter of a century later with regard to the Caernarvon firm of de Winton.) Both identical, they were built and delivered, almost certainly by sea, in 1848 and bore the names *Fire Queen* and *Jenny Lind*. They carried no works numbers.

The design is directly attributable to T. R. Crampton, the then designer for the firm of G. & J. Rennie. Basically it was an 0-4-0 tender engine design with a remarkably long wheelbase of 12ft 0½in; Crampton's design made provision for an intermediate axle and dummy cranks to take the strain off the long coupling rods though this modification was not fitted to the Padarn locomotives—with the resulting effect that the coupling rods frequently buckled! There was no framing: the leading axle guards were brackets riveted directly to the boiler shell (which was lagged with wooden strips). The trailing axle guards were similar brackets riveted to the front plate of the firebox. The boiler was 8ft 3½in long and the wheels 4ft 6in in diameter. Suspension was by means of 4½in diameter spiral springs of 1in square section.

The motion was transmitted from the two outside cylinders inclined high up on massive boiler mountings behind the leading wheels to the rear axle. The leading axle carried the eccentrics to operate the Stephenson valve gear back to a shaft in front of the firebox. From here it was connected to the valves above the cylinders. The 13in x 22in cylinders were fed with steam at 60lb/sq in from the boiler which was set off by a towering 13in diameter chimney.

The tender was a simple four-wheeled affair with 3ft 6in diameter wheels at 7ft 9½in centres and carried the coke used as fuel. Hand-operated wooden brake shoes on the wheels comprised the only brake on the locomotive, in accordance with contemporary practice. The total length of the locomotive over buffers was 33ft 10in and 2ft less over the buffer beams. The buffers themselves were of a type known as 'Bradley's Patent' and utilised rubber and leather pads.

When delivered neither engine was equipped with a cab,

again normal practice at that time, though one was later fitted to *Jenny Lind*—strong evidence that this was the engine which saw the most use in later years. The design, doubtless adequate at first for the amount of traffic, soon proved unable to cope and in the 1880s was replaced by a far more modern and efficient one. From the delivery dates of these replacement locomotives it appears that *Jenny Lind* was scrapped in 1886 (the brass safety valve and dome cover survived to the 1969 auction that followed the closure of the Dinorwic Quarry) while *Fire Queen* had probably been withdrawn four years earlier as her boiler was in poor condition. The latter engine was placed in store in a tiny private museum at the quarry works; a visitor in 1905 described its livery (presumably its working colours) as green boiler cladding, brown undergear and tender frame, black smokebox and chimney and vermilion buffer beams. With the final closure of the quarry in 1969 it was moved to the National Trust museum at Penrhyn Castle.

*The Hunslets*

The replacements for the outdated Horlocks were, not very surprisingly, ordered from the Hunslet Engine Co of Leeds, the constructors of the narrow gauge quarry and port locomotives. They emerged from the works as identical 0-6-0 side tank engines:

| Name | Works no | Year |
|---|---|---|
| Dinorwic | 302 | 1882 |
| Pandora | 410 | 1886 |
| Velinheli | 631 | 1895 |

These engines had $12\frac{1}{2}$in x 20in outside cylinders driving 3ft 6in wheels. The total wheelbase was 10ft. The tractive effort at 75 per cent boiler pressure was 7812lb. Steam pressure was 140lb.

*Dinorwic* and *Pandora* were intended as replacements for the Horlock engines and took over both the original locomotives' duties in 1886. The need for an extra engine later became apparent and consequently *Velinheli* was supplied. This last engine had cast steel wheel centres in contrast to the others' wrought iron ones but apart from this technical improvement it was identical to its two predecessors.

In May 1909 the name *Pandora* was changed to *Amalthaea* and in 1930 new wheels were fitted, this work being carried out at the quarry workshops where the overhauls and repairs were performed. Normally only one engine was required to work the line, leaving one at the quarry as a spare in case of extra traffic on the line. This arrangement was not a foolproof one since major overhauls meant that one locomotive might be out of work for a considerable period of time—hence the purchase of *Velinheli*. The success of this arrangement of one in use, one in shed and one in the works can be judged by the fact that it survived virtually intact right up to the closing of the railway. The standby engine was kept at Gilfach Ddu and the one in current service was shedded at Penscoins from where it operated the morning workmen's train to the quarry, returning on a similar errand in the evening. The engines could be uncoupled automatically from their trains by means of a lever on the footplate. In 1920 Hunslets prepared plans for converting all three locomotives to oil-firing, using a Kermode's 'Onchan' burner, but nothing came of the proposal.

The livery scheme used on all three engines was similar to that later borne by the LMS passenger locomotives on the neighbouring Llanberis branch, being crimson bodywork with black edging and yellow lining.

*The Hardy*

The line's last locomotive, its sixth, was a four-wheeled petrol-engined machine built for the railway by Hardy Motors Ltd of Slough, Bucks. Constructed in 1925 as works no 954 it was intended for use in a very general capacity, such as shunting at Gilfach Ddu, or in situations where its special advantages would be of importance, eg going to breakdowns or taking over services at short notice. It was fitted with a 55hp four cylinder engine with a large tubular type radiator at either end of the body. A four-speed gearbox gave running speeds of approximately 2½mph, 4mph, 8mph and 16mph in either direction, thus enabling it to work scheduled slate trains along the railway.

The transmission was taken mechanically to each axle from the gearbox, at the rear of which was fitted a foot-operated band brake. A second brake operated via cast iron shoes on all four wheels and was controlled by a screw wheel. The unsymmetrical bodywork consisted of a large cab and the engine and radiator covers; ballast boxes were incorporated into the design in order to raise the weight to twelve tons to provide enough adhesion. The driver stood sideways to the cab controls, thus enabling him to observe the road when running in either direction. A further refinement on the locomotive which greatly added to its usefulness was a winding drum with 250ft of steel cable below the engine, operating in both directions, and complete with horizontal capstans on either end of the winding shaft. The livery carried was identical to that of its steam companions.

It is slightly ironic that *Velinheli*, the last of the three Hunslets to arrive, should have been the first to go. In November 1953 it was stripped down in the workshops for a major overhaul and, such was the uncertainty over the whole future of the line, it remained in that state for ten years until April 1963 when it was scrapped by Pittrail Ltd, together with the *Hardy*. *Dinorwic* and *Amalthaea* survived them by only four months before suffering a similar fate.

PASSENGER STOCK

*Quarrymen's carriages*

These vehicles were constructed by the Gloucester Railway Carriage & Waggon Co Ltd in 1895 for the Padarn Railway. The original order was for fifteen carriages each capable of holding sixty workmen and four brake carriages to seat fifty-eight; this was later increased to nineteen and four respectively. Each ran on four spoked wheels (2ft 4in diameter) set at 9ft 6in centres with an underframe length of 22ft. Overall width was 7ft 9in and the height (to the top of the lamp covers) 10ft 9in. The bodywork was made of oak, with a deal roof. Low internal partitions divided the coach into six compartments: the back-to-back cross-benches each seated five persons, making a total of sixty. Two oil lamps provided internal lighting. The brake carriages were similar with the small difference of a screw brake wheel taking up seating space for two workmen.

The quarry specifications (given on 4 March 1895) included 2in high white figures inside for every seat and 6in high white letters outside, giving the station served by the coach, and a 6in white number. This was however changed to a letter, the carriages being labelled in the series A-W inclusive. They were also to be given a final coat of paint of the same colour and quality as that used on the Midland Railway passenger stock. Delivery was via the LNWR to Llanberis, thence by road to Gilfach Ddu.

By 1942 only three coaches, K, Q and U were in active service, the others having been withdrawn and probably scrapped. These last three were withdrawn in 1947 following the termination of the workmen's train service but they lingered on for several years until vanishing with the closure of the railway in 1961.

*The saloon*

The Padarn Railway owned a private saloon for the use of the quarry owner and his guests. This was constructed in 1896 by the Gloucester Railway Carriage & Waggon Co and had identical running gear and overall dimensions to the quarrymen's vehicles. It was naturally far more splendid in appearance, both inside and out, with varnished teak bodywork (complete with coat of arms in the centre) and eight padded revolving chairs. Additional seating was supplied by four flap seats on one end platform and three on the other where the brake wheel was sited. (These end platforms were verandahs partitioned off from the saloon proper.) The underframes were of oak and the body was mounted on thick rubber blocks. These specifications were finally agreed to by the quarry management on 13 December 1895 and it too was delivered to Llanberis by the LNWR.

In 1953 the carriage was painted bright red with black lining

Page 141:
(above) Jubilee 1897: Manning, Wardle 1382 of 1897, arrived Penrhyn Quarry August 1928; (below) also arrived August 1928, the only secondhand Hunslet at Penrhyn, Lilla (554/1891)

Page 142:
(above) *Penrhyn Quarry's foreigner*: Orenstein & Koppel Eigiau (5668/1912) *acquired 1929;* (below) *Kerr, Stuart 2395 of 1917,* Stanhope. *Purchased 1934, moved from Port Penrhyn to the quarry in 1940 and withdrawn seven years later*

and used to bring the workmen's pay up from the port—under armed guard! It was withdrawn in 1960 and nine years later accompanied *Fire Queen* to Penrhyn Castle.

### GOODS STOCK

*Early waggons*

The original waggons used on the railway—or more correctly tramroad—were described in the 1842 contracts as 'Large Trucks for Slates'. They were horse drawn and weighed 6½cwt. In all eighty-seven such waggons were ordered, in lots of twelve or thirteen, from a number of local contractors. They were made of iron and were probably simply a larger design of the quarry waggons then in use, bearing in mind that they had to be easily loaded and unloaded by hand. Little else is known about them and unfortunately no examples survive.

*Transporters*

There were in all eighty-four transporter waggons built for the working of locomotive-hauled trains. These were fitted with dumb buffers on wooden frames. Originally the brake consisted of semi-circular steel bands on the upper half of the wheels, operated by a pedal on the waggon floor. These were replaced in the 1940s with conventional shoe type brakes operated by a side lever when the waggons went into the workshops for repair. They were constructed in the Gilfach Ddu works as an ingenious solution to the transhipment problem: the bodywork consisted of a flat wooden platform through which the tops of the four wheels protruded; on this platform two sets of 1ft 10¾in gauge rails were laid longitudinally, the outer rails being positioned outside the transporter wheels.

*Other waggons*

The only other waggons owned by the Padarn Railway were two ballast waggons about which little is known. They may possibly have been adapted from two of the early slate trucks.

I

## VELOCIPEDES

The velocipedes were of two types: worked by foot treadle or by hand cranks. Each was built and operated by a syndicate of quarrymen. The hand-propelled machines held eight passengers while the foot-powered machines could hold twice that number. They were simply constructed with wooden frames and four large, spoked, metal wheels of very light construction. A one seater velocipede also existed, made from a bicycle. This would most probably have been used as an inspection trolley.

An 1893 list of fifty-two velocipedes survives, naming all of them, although in 1901 only six were left and in 1904 only four. One wonders which, if any, out of such vehicles as *Duke of Wellington, Victoria, Stanley, Livingstone, Prince of Wales, Stag, Fox, Jennie Bach, Black Bess, Pandora, Snowdon, Arfonia, Eryri* and *Padarn* still bore their names with pride. The velocipedes were known in Welsh as *ceir gwylltion* (wild cars), no doubt because of their turn of speed, but are not to be confused with the similarly named man-riding incline sleds used in other North Wales quarries.

Padarn Railway velocipede permit. (Reverse blank)

CHAPTER 7

# Dinorwic Stock

### LOCOMOTIVES

For the sake of convenience the Dinorwic locomotives (ie those that worked in the quarry complex or at Port Dinorwic) can be easily divided into five main groups: the Hunslet Mills class; the Hunslet Port class; the Hunslet Alice class; the 'outsiders' (the remaining varied collection of steam engines) and the internal combustion locomotives. Each locomotive was originally purchased for a pre-determined purpose and set to work in a specific locality, eg at the port or on a certain level in the quarry, and usually remained there for a considerable period of time. This was done for the very good reason of obviating the wasteful task of hauling locomotives up and down inclines in order for them to work different galleries. This pattern was not, however, a rigid one, nor could it ever be; for while routine maintenance could be carried out in the gallery, heavy repairs meant that the locomotive had to be taken down to the workshops at Gilfach Ddu. At such times a replacement engine would be sent up to fill the gap and the repaired locomotive would then serve as a replacement for one from a different level, and so on: a sort of 'Musical Galleries'! Thus any statement as to where a particular engine worked is often only valid if the actual period it did so is specified.

At the end of their working life the engines were either sold for work elsewhere (a rare occurrence) and thus removed from the quarry, or simply left derelict on their own level until someone appeared who was willing to buy one for preservation. Then—and only then—would it be worth the effort of bringing it down to the bottom level. By the beginning of 1963 only four steam locomotives were still in active service. These were *Holy War, Maid Marian, Dolbadarn* and *Sybil*.

Apart from this unceasing rotation of locomotives, another fact which tends to make life somewhat exasperating for the historian is that the actual identity of any one locomotive is by no means a straightforward matter. Not content with chopping and changing the numbers and/or names (often resulting in duplication of identities at different dates) the quarry company regarded all replaceable parts as belonging to a common pool for reasons of efficiency and the ease of repair. Thus after a few sessions in the works only the frames would retain the 'true' identity of an engine: boiler, tank, cylinders and all the other various removable pieces all originating either from a different locomotive or else as spares from the manufacturers. (There were in fact more boilers than locomotives in existence, these being numbered in a separate series.) Under this system a malfunctioning part of one of the Hunslet locomotives could be removed and replaced very quickly, enabling it to resume its everyday duties while the removed item could be repaired at leisure. The livery scheme was the same as that of the Padarn Railway engines; the steam locomotives were named after topographical features of the locality, members of the Assheton-Smith family or their racehorses.

In the following sections the individual locomotive notes are preceded by the name or number carried at the time of disposal. All, unless otherwise specifically stated, were purchased new from the manufacturer.

#### MILLS CLASS

This class of Hunslet locomotives (class word Vanol) comprised only two engines which were used solely, as far as is known, on the Gilfach Ddu level of the quarry. Consequently

DINORWIC STOCK 147

they were known in the quarry as the 'tramway' locomotives. Their design was an 0-4-0 saddle tank engine with 26in wheels and 8½in x 14in cylinders. Weight in working order was 11¾ tons and the tractive effort developed at 75 per cent boiler pressure (140lb/sq in) was 4085lb. They were the heaviest and the most powerful of the Hunslet engines used in the quarry and performed the hardest work—shunting the loaded slate waggons ready for transporting over the Padarn Railway. In their appearance they were set apart from the other Hunslets by their size, safety valves positioned on the steam dome and a dropped frame at the rear of the engine upon which was mounted an overall cab. (Regarding the question of cabs on the other locomotives, it appears that these were not usually fitted owing to the restricted loading gauge of most of the galleries; they could, however, be fitted on the locomotives at the port or on those purchased secondhand complete with cabs. Once again, cabs were regarded as 'common'). More detailed statistics of these and the other Hunslet classes of locomotives are listed in Appendix 5. Individually, they were:

*'Jerry M'*

Built by the Hunslet Engine Co of Leeds as order number 17830 and despatched on 20 September 1895, as works number 638, this engine was originally named *Vaenol*. The name was not changed until 1908 or later. It was sold in 1967 and is now preserved.

*'Cackler'*

Built in 1898 as Hunslet 671 (order no 19860), it was originally named *Port Dinorwic*, again until 1908 or later. It was despatched from Leeds on 11 May 1898 and used from the start on the bottom level. On 29 March 1966 it was sent from the quarry to D. C. Potter & Co Ltd, Dereham, Norfolk, who had purchased it for display.

PORT CLASS

This class comprised three locomotives, these being the last three Hunslets to arrive at Dinorwic. They were smaller and less powerful than their predecessors the Mills class, having 20in wheels and 7in x 10in cylinders. Again they were 0-4-0 saddle tanks with outside cylinders (class word Dinor). Tractive effort was 2940lb at 75 per cent of the boiler pressure. In overall dimensions they were smaller than the Mills class and did not have the latter's dropped frame at the rear. They did however have a domed boiler with the safety valves mounted on the dome, a smaller version of that used on the Mills class locomotives. As constructed they were equipped with spring buffers (a luxury not enjoyed by the Mills class) but these were later removed and replaced by wooden dumb ones.

As their name implies the first two of the trio were used for shunting on the quay at Port Dinorwic, though they remained there for different lengths of time, and sported overall cabs.

*No 1*

This was Hunslet 1429 of 1922, despatched 1 August, order no 40830, and as delivered bore the number 1. Some time prior to 1945 the number was removed and the engine was named *Lady Joan*. At a still later date it reverted back to its original identity. By 1967 it had been withdrawn from service and was then sold for preservation. It appears to have carried its cab for the major part of its life. At one time it was fitted with a chimney 12in taller than the original class design.

*'Dolbadarn'*

Sister engine to No 1, Hunslet 1430 of 1922 (despatched 11 August), it was originally identified as No 2. In October 1935 it was transferred from the port to the quarry, having been replaced by a diesel locomotive. At its new location the cab was removed and from 23 November 1945 was known as *Dolbadarn*. In November 1950 it was reboiled with an Alice class boiler, the old one becoming a stationary boiler in the Gilfach Ddu workshops. It was withdrawn from service in 1967, one of the last steam locomotives to work at Dinorwic, and sold for preservation in the 1969 auction.

## 'Michael'

The last engine of the trio was Hunslet 1709, order no 46240, built in 1932 and despatched on 27 September for work in the quarry, not at the port. By 1963 it was out of use and stored in a shed on the Duffryn gallery, its last working place. Two years later, in June 1965, it was sold and sent to Canada.

### ALICE CLASS

This remaining class of Hunslets consisted of no less than thirteen locomotives and formed the main body of the steam work force in the quarry. (The four other Hunslets which worked on the system at one time or another will be considered with the rest of the outsiders.) Again 0-4-0 saddle tanks with outside cylinders and frames (class word Velin), the Alice class was similar in design to the Port class but with a lower pitched, domeless boiler. They were ideally suited to working the light, winding tracks in the quarry complex, helped in this by the fact that they were cabless. As with all the other 1ft 10¾in gauge engines one-man operation was the norm. As constructed they were fitted with wooden dumb buffers.

Reference has been made in the previous chapter to the 1920 plans to equip the Padarn Hunslets with oil burning apparatus. Similar plans were also prepared (dated 19 October) for equipping the Alice class engines with a Kermode's Patent 'Galva' oil burner, to accommodate which part of the frame would have had to be cut away. Cost of the conversion, including burner, oil tank, valves and firebricks was put at £120 10s per engine. Nothing however came of this interesting scheme which would have set the precedent for present-day steam working on the Festiniog Railway.

## 'Velinheli'

Hunslet 409, order no 9170, this engine was constructed in 1886 and despatched 9 October; withdrawn by 1962 it was later sold for preservation.

## 'King of the Scarlets'

Hunslet 492, order no 11550, constructed in 1889 and

despatched 12 November, this originally carried the name *Alice* until at least 1908. In April 1947 it was reboilered with boiler no 25 and a new steel firebox fitted. (This history is typical of the class.) On 1 May it was put to work on the Dyffryn gallery. On 7 April 1958 further repairs were performed when the steel smoke tubes were renewed. In October 1960 the cylinders were rebored, new piston heads and rings fitted, the slide valve seatings machined, new valves ground in, the valve motion reconditioned and new pins fitted. It returned to work on the Dyffryn level until 7 January 1962 when it was damaged in a rock fall and taken out of service. It remained in the same shed as *Michael* until June 1965 when it accompanied its stablemate to Canada.

'Red Damsel'

Sister engine to *King of the Scarlets*, this was Hunslet 493 of 1889, despatched 28 October. The original name was *Enid*, until at least 1908. (Both *Alice* and *Enid* were renamed by 1945.) It ended its working life at the very top of the quarry and was dismantled in November 1957 for overhaul, never being reassembled. It was kept in store until the auction of 1969 when it was sold for preservation. Both 492 and 493 were fitted with shorter chimneys to give a height of only 6ft 6in compared with 7ft 2in for the rest of the class.

'Rough Pup'

Formerly No 1 until at least 1908, Hunslet 541 of 1891 (order no 13300, despatched 8 June) also finished its service in the upper levels (on the Pen Garret gallery); it was withdrawn by 1960. In non-operational order, it was later presented to the Narrow Gauge Railway Museum at Towyn and was removed from the quarry on 15 June 1968.

'Cloister'

Hunslet 542 of 1891 (sister engine to *Rough Pup*), this was the original No 2 in the quarry list, again until at least 1908. It was sold for preservation in August 1962.

'Bernstein'

Built in 1898 as Hunslet 678, order no 20700, despatched

20 August, *Bernstein* (then named *The First*) was used at Port Dinorwic until the arrival of the Port class engines in 1922. Its original name implies that it was the first locomotive to be used on the quay lines. Presumably in 1922 it was removed to the quarry where it worked till its withdrawal, ending its days on the Pen Garret level. In July 1967 it was sold for preservation.

*'Covertcoat'*

Hunslet 679 of 1898, sister engine to *Bernstein* and despatched on 26 November, this was logically named *The Second*. It had a similar history to no 678 and was sold in December 1964 for preservation.

*'George B'*

Originally named *Wellington*, Hunslet 680 of 1898 (same order no as the two above and despatched 17 October) appears to have completed a trio of engines which all worked at the port for the first years of their life. Later it worked in the quarry and was eventually sold for preservation in October 1965.

*'Holy War'*

Hunslet 779 of 1902, order no 24820 and despatched 29 May, this engine continued the number sequence in the quarry begun in 1891 with the original Nos 1 and 2 (see above) by becoming No 3. (It should be noted in passing that these numbers were not simply numerals but brass plates carried on the saddle tanks, as were the names, bearing the legend 'No 3' or whatever it was.) This number lasted until 1908 when alongside the number in the quarry stock list *Holy War* is noted in brackets. It remained in service until the end of 1967, on the Penrhydd Bach gallery, winning for itself the distinction of being the last steam locomotive to work on the entire system. It was subsequently sold for preservation in 1968.

*'Alice'*

Also constructed in 1902, as Hunslet 780, *Alice* was the

sister engine to the above locomotive. Despatched from Leeds on 16 June it carried the identity No 4 until at least 1908. It was withdrawn in February 1961 and was left abandoned on the Australia level. It was possibly stripped of certain parts as spares for other locomotives before it was sold to a private purchaser who, deciding that restoration was impractical, stripped it of all re-usable parts. The remains lay derelict in the gallery until 1972 when, minus wheels, it was lowered on a waggon chassis (a trip taking several months to complete) down the derelict inclines and removed for restoration.

'Maid Marian'

Hunslet 822 of 1903, order no 26000 and despatched 2 October, this engine was set to work originally in the Allt Ddu section of the quarry as No 5. One of the last four steam locomotives remaining in service in 1963, it was withdrawn by 1964, stored in the Pen Garret gallery shed and sold for preservation in 1966 to the Maid Marian Locomotive Fund which had been set up to prevent the engine from being purchased by a foreign buyer. It was transferred to the Bressingham Steam Museum at Diss but later moved again 'back home' to the Llanberis Lake Railway (see Chapter 8).

'Irish Mail'

Hunslet 823 of 1903, despatched 30 October, *Irish Mail* was the sister engine to the above locomotive. It began life as No 6 in the quarry list, on the Pen Garret level. In July 1959 it was taken out of service and the boiler removed. It remained in that condition for ten years until the 1969 auction when it was sold for preservation.

'Wild Aster'

Originally No 7, this was the last of the Alice class to be ordered (order no 26980) and was despatched on 13 June 1904 as Hunslet 849. It joined No 6 on the Pen Garret gallery and was likewise sold for preservation in the 1969 auction, having been withdrawn eight years previously as unfit for service.

OTHERS

The Dinorwic system operated at various dates, in addition to the three classes of Hunslets described above, at least eight other steam locomotives of several differing designs and builders. Four were from the Hunslet Engine Co; the others were from four separate firms. Three of the 'outsiders' were purchased secondhand for use in the quarry. In chronological order of construction the locomotives were:

*'Charlie'*

Formerly named *Dinorwic* (until a date before 1901), this was Hunslet 51 of 1870, order no 670. It was probably the first locomotive to work in the quarry. As regards wheel, tank and cylinder arrangements it was similar in design to all the other Hunslets. It had 7½in x 14in cylinders and 24in wheels. It was withdrawn in 1916 and stored in the works until it was scrapped c1940.

*The de Wintons*

The only de Winton known to have definitely worked at Dinorwic is *Wellington*, an 0-4-0 tank engine with a vertical boiler and vertically placed cylinders—the 'standard' design for quarry locomotives from this builder. No date of construction can be safely given but it was certainly contemporary with the Penrhyn de Wintons (see Chapter 5) and possibly dated from as early as 1870. It is likely that it worked the bottom level line at Gilfach Ddu, along with the locomotive listed above, until 1895 at the latest when it was moved to the Vivian section of the quarry upon the arrival of *Vaenol* (later *Jerry M*). By the end of the nineteenth century it had been sold and moved across Llyn Padarn to the small Glynrhonwy Slate Quarry just down the lake from Llanberis. It was scrapped there about the time of World War I.

Three other de Wintons are believed to have worked in the quarry: *Harriet*, *Peris* and *Victoria*. From what little is known about them they hardly qualify for the description of 'locomotives'. Fitted with only a single cylinder and double flanged wheels for negotiating the temporary trackwork to the rock face, they were little more than self-propelled power units for the rock drills. Presumably they too had simple vertical boilers.

### 'George'

This was another early Hunslet, 184 of 1877, order no 3060, and appears to have been similar in design to *Charlie* in respect of wheels and cylinders. Again it was an 0-4-0 saddle tank. It was withdrawn in 1916 and sold to S. Fletcher of Halifax, a dealer, in 1919 and from there passed to a Shropshire mining company.

### 'Louisa'

Another Hunslet 0-4-0 saddle tank, this was 195 of 1877, order no 3390. It was a smaller version of the other Hunslets with 5in x 8in cylinders and only 18in wheels. Other principal dimensions were:

| | |
|---|---|
| Wheelbase: | 3ft 0in |
| Water capacity: | 60gal |
| Fuel capacity: | 3¾cu ft |
| Total heating surface: | 56sq ft |
| Grate area: | 1¼sq ft |
| Weight empty: | 3tons 6cwt |
| Weight loaded: | 3tons 18cwt |
| Tractive effort: | 1,000lb |

It accompanied de Winton *Wellington* c1898 to the Glynrhonwy quarry and was later scrapped there.

### 'Lady Madcap'

Originally named *Elidir* when it first worked at Dinorwic, *Lady Madcap* had begun life as Hunslet 0-4-0 saddle tank, 652 of 1896. Built for a gauge of 2ft, it had worked at Groby Granite Co, Leics (carrying the name *Sextus*), before returning to the manufacturers who rebuilt it, regauged it to 1ft 10¾in and sold it to Dinorwic in 1910. The rebuilding appears to have been simply a matter of removing the cab roof and its four supporting pillars. It remained at Dinorwic for the rest of its working days. It had 7in x 10in cylinders, 20¼in wheels, a 4ft 0in wheelbase and a dropped footplate at the rear. Otherwise it was somewhat similar to the Alice class engines and indeed was adapted in 1931 to take a boiler of this design. In March 1952 it was taken out of service for the last time and doubtless cannibalised before the remains were scrapped.

'Sybil'

Built in 1906, *Sybil* was an 0-4-0 saddle tank constructed by W. G. Bagnall Ltd, Stafford, as works no 1760. It had 7in x 12in outside cylinders, 21½in wheels and a 3ft 6in wheelbase. Weight in working order was 7tons 15cwt. It commenced work on the Anglesey level and was still active in 1963. Later it was withdrawn and sold for preservation.

No 70

This curiously numbered locomotive was constructed by Andrew Barclay Sons & Co, Kilmarnock, in 1931. Works no 1995, No 70 was an 0-4-0 well tank with outside cylinders and an overall cab. Leading dimensions were:

| | |
|---|---|
| Wheel Diameter: | 1ft 10in |
| Wheelbase: | 3ft 11½in |
| Cylinders: | 7in x 11in |
| Boiler pressure: | 180lb/sq in |
| Weight in working order: | 7tons 10cwt |

It was a secondhand purchase, having been built as a 2ft gauge engine and later used at Raisby Quarries Ltd, County Durham, from whence it arrived in 1948. It was regauged at Gilfach Ddu. No 70 was sold for preservation in August 1962.

'Elidir'

Avonside Engine Co, Bristol, 2071 of 1933, *Elidir* was an 0-4-0 side tank engine with outside cylinders and an overall cab. Originally another 2ft gauge locomotive, *Elidir* arrived in July 1949 from R. Dunn, a Bishop Auckland dealer; it was the last steam engine to be bought for the quarry. Prior to 1949 it was owned by Blythe & Sons (Birtley) Ltd of County Durham. Its main dimensions were:

Wheel diameter:         2ft 0in
Wheelbase:              3ft 9in
Cylinders:              7½in × 12in
Boiler pressure:        180lb/sq in
Weight in working order: 7tons 10cwt

After withdrawal it was sold for preservation and left for Canada on 20 July 1966.

### INTERNAL COMBUSTION

As has been mentioned elsewhere, internal combustion locomotives were introduced in the Dinorwic system from 1935 onwards at an increasing rate. This is hardly surprising for this pattern of events was repeated on countless other industrial systems throughout the British Isles. What *is* interesting is the fact that they did not succeed in replacing steam traction: both forms of motive power were actually run down together during the 1950s and 1960s. Between 1935 and 1957 twenty-one diesel locomotives and one petrol locomotive were purchased, either new or secondhand, for use in the quarry or at Port Dinorwic. They were allocated numbers which corresponded to those of the levels on which they first worked but the high level of cannibalisation which took place, together with movements to different galleries, often resulted in these numbers being altered in later years. (Appendix 6 gives the complete stock list of these locomotives.)

The first withdrawal took place in 1954. More followed as the quarry railways were gradually replaced by road vehicles and by 1967 only five internal combustion locomotives were in active use, the rest having been either scrapped, dismantled for spares or simply placed in store. (Just four years before there had been no less than eighteen at work.) By the time of the auction in December 1969 only one survived in more or less operational order; this now runs on the Llanberis Lake Railway. Two others survive in the quarry in a derelict condition; the other eighteen have all been scrapped.

## ROLLING STOCK

### Passenger stock

Though not strictly 'passenger' stock, the Dinorwic Quarry built and operated five vehicles for the use of visitors to the quarry. These were known as incline carriages because they were towed up the inclines to the galleries when in use for a tour of the workings. The seats were angled slightly for the comfort of the passengers while this was happening. The first three were built at an unknown date and the last two early in 1899 for the royal visit of that year. All were of wooden construction, the early design having four simple bench seats (each holding two passengers) atop a wooden frame, the later design having bodywork as high as the seat backs with access openings on either side. (This design was very similar, though on a smaller scale, to that of the Penrhyn quarrymen's carriages. See Chapter 5.) All had four wheels; the 1899 carriages had bright yellow exteriors, black interiors and removable cushions. The last two constructed, and one of the earlier models, survived till the closure of the quarry.

### Goods stock

The 'goods stock' used on the Dinorwic system falls into a number of different categories, the two major ones in numerical terms being the waste waggons and the slate waggons. The waste, or rubbish, waggons were used solely in the quarry and, as their name implies, served to carry away waste rock from the working area for dumping elsewhere. They also appear to have been used to carry slate blocks to the dressing sheds since the quarry did not possess a fleet of more specialised waggons for this purpose. Manufactured (as indeed were all the Dinorwic waggons) in the quarry workshops from ¼in mild steel plate, a typical body was 4ft 6in long, 3ft wide, 1ft 4in deep and held 2 tons of stone. It ran on four double-flanged wheels of about 15in diameter and 2ft 2in wheelbase; the wheels were loose on the axles so as to negotiate sharp curves and rough trackwork in general. Each waggon had one end completely open to allow easy loading and unloading. In 1906 there were over 1300 of these waggons in use though this number was a very fluid one since the quarry waggons were often cannibalised or scrapped when damaged and new ones constructed when needed.

The slate waggons were used to convey the finished slates from the dressing sheds to Port Dinorwic and had slightly smaller bodies than the rubbish waggons. They were constructed of wooden bars and cast iron distance pieces to give a light framework of a body which could hold 2 tons of slate—the dressed slates were stacked upright across the floor and packed in tightly with a large wooden mallet to prevent breakage en route. The double-flanged wheels on these trucks were fitted on to stub axles, each held in two bearings, as conventional axles would have fouled the tops of the wheels on the transporters. The highest total for these waggons was 627 in 1906 but possibly more (unrecorded) existed at other times.

The next group of trucks falls a long way short of this: in 1905 the quarry was recorded as having fourteen slab waggons. These were simply flat waggons on to which slabs of slate could be chained. There were slightly fewer timber waggons which apparently consisted of an open metal frame and back (5ft 1in long by 3ft wide) for carrying baulks of timber around the quarry if needed. Finally there were the

Page 159:
(above) Dolbadarn *at Gilfach Ddu on the Llanberis Lake Railway, 1973;* (below) *Penscoins, looking towards the incline head, 1973. The white building on the left is the former shed for Assheton-Smith's saloon. Now a private house, the 1896 date is still visible over the original doorway*

Page 160:
(above) *Penllyn level crossing, 1973. The keeper's hut is identical to the others on the line;* (right) *1896 Pontrhythallt carriage shed, 1973. Note stile made from old rails;* (below) *1895 Penscoins engine shed, 1973. Sheet iron water tank and coal bunker supported by the ubiquitous old rails*

three guards vans for use on the Padarn Railway. One of these would travel on the last transporter in the train, along with three slate waggons, and in this the guard would sit—just! To enable it to fit on to the transporter it had to be the same size as a slate waggon, though naturally somewhat taller, with an enclosed wooden body and an end door. Again, these vehicles had stub axles for the reason mentioned.

All vehicles were equipped with hook and chain couplers which were also used to attach them to the inclines; none were braked. In later years they were 'natural' coloured in appearance though this had not always been the case—an early specification for a rubbish waggon states that it was to have one coat of 'best lead colour oil paint' and a second of 'purple brown paint of best quality'.

CHAPTER 8

## *Today*

### THE LLANBERIS LAKE RAILWAY

Beside Llyn Padarn a new pleasure line has been laid on the site of the old Padarn Railway. On 25 April 1970 a meeting was held to consider the possibility of this undertaking; it met with considerable support. It was decided to run the new railway as a commercial venture, as opposed to a preservation scheme, needing the financial support of a body of shareholders —£10 being the minimum amount accepted. Mr A. Lowry Porter was elected chairman of the Llanberis Lake Railway Company Ltd. The closing of the quarry had caused much hardship in the area so it was hoped that this new tourist attraction would help bring some employment to the district.

At this early stage plans were made for the laying of a two mile stretch of 1ft 10¾in gauge track on the 4ft gauge trackbed northwards from Gilfach Ddu. Its name, the Llanberis Lake Railway, and its gauge were soon both to undergo a slight change. By October 1970 the official Welsh name of Rheilffordd Llyn Llanberis had been adopted although the railway is also still known by the English title. Rapid progress was being made: Mr Porter's ex-Dinorwic locomotives were being overhauled and fifteen 60cm gauge side-tipping bogie waggons were acquired from W. R. Cunis Ltd of Rainham, Essex. The *Guardian* of 30 December 1970 reported that approximately £20,000 had been raised and plans had been made to have the first 1¼ mile section in operation by 28 May,

Spring Holiday Saturday, 1971. Tracklaying began that December. Six coaches, some open and some closed, were undergoing construction in the old quarry workshops on the frames of the ex-Cunis waggons; this work, the locomotive overhauling and the tracklaying were under the supervision of the manager Mr V. J. Bradley. The track gauge was at this point altered to 1ft 11½in—the logic of this move being that it would be easier to regauge the locomotives to this more 'standard' 2ft gauge than to regauge all the existing rolling stock.

Some of the track was laid with chaired double-headed rail from the Dinorwic Quarry and some with flat-bottom rail from the North Devon Clay Co. Dinorwic type stub points were installed in the works yard but conventional points were laid where passenger trains would run. The ex-Dinorwic locomotives were joined by two Motor Rail diesels (5861 and 21513) from Birmingham Corporation Water Works and were numbered 5 and 6. (The ex-Dinorwic Ruston was No 4.) The railway did not open to the public on the inauguration day of 28 May: the essential brake van could not be delivered in time for the opening and a replacement had to be hurriedly constructed, taking up the time needed to run-in the track. Mr Bradley, in a letter to the *Caernarvon & Denbigh Herald* the following week takes up the story:

> On the day of the official opening, we devoted the morning to the operation of test trains, and it was during these tests that a passenger coach came off the track. As all previous tests had been satisfactory, a thorough investigation was immediately started to ascertain the cause of the mishap. It was found that the weight of the steam locomotive had caused the track to settle slightly into the new ballast chippings, and that the coach was too rigid to ride in safety over this settlement. . . .
>
> Later a very careful check of the line confirmed that it was perfectly safe, and so we ran a special train for a pre-booked party (members of the North Wales Railway Circle) the following day. No more trains will be run for a few weeks, however, as we intend to ensure that no further

undue settlement of the ballast can occur; we are also making some modifications to the coaches in order that they will be more flexible, and thus more readily accommodate any irregularities in the line.

Two further Motor Rails (7902 and 7927) arrived at this time; both were 6 ton 40hp Simplex diesels from Murex Ltd, Rainham. No 5 had meanwhile been converted into a brake van. The new arrivals became No 7 *Garrett* and No 8 *Braich* respectively. The railway eventually opened to the public on 19 July and inauguration speeches were made by Mr Porter and Mr T. Mervyn Jones, chairman of the Wales Tourist Board. The three coaches then completed were smartly painted green and cream, with varnished wood interiors, and the locomotive *Dolbadarn* Dinorwic maroon. The return fare to the temporary terminus at Cei Llydan ($1\frac{1}{4}$ miles) and back was 25p and in the first fourteen days of operation more than 6000 tickets were sold. Platforms, booking office and water columns had been constructed or adapted and a large site cleared for use as a car park. The 1971 timetable gave a 45 minute service daily until 3 October.

During its first three month season the Llanberis Lake Railway carried 30,500 passengers. After October work progressed to complete the two mile long railway and by February 1972 the remainder of the lakeside route to the terminus at Penllyn had been cleared of undergrowth. New 50lb rails were laid and the line ballasted with clean grade stone, over 1000 tons having been delivered from the Dinmor Quarry on Anglesey. New points were installed to increase passenger comfort. The former fitting shop at Gilfach Ddu underwent conversion into a well-equipped workshop for servicing the line's stock. The 1971 season had been worked by No 3 *Dolbadarn* and No 4 *Chwarelwr* ('Quarryman'); *Dolbadarn* was now joined by the renovated No 1 *Elidir* (ex-Dinorwic *Red Damsel* with a cab taken from *Irish Mail*). During exceedingly busy periods these two were aided by *Maid Marian* which had returned from Bressingham on 25 October 1971. No 2 *Wild Aster* was still undergoing extensive repairs. A fifth steam locomotive

*Cyclops* (Jung 7509 of 1937), an 0-4-0 well tank from Germany, was also under repair, on loan to the line. The number of coaches was increased to nine; the doors are fitted on the Gilfach Ddu platform side only since the lake on the other side comes right to the track edge at several places. Services were resumed in May 1972 with the opening of the second and final section to Penllyn. The coach fleet in 1973 stood at twelve, with a variety of bodies and chassis but all with bogies and running gear designed and manufactured at Gilfach Ddu.

### THE NORTH WALES QUARRYING MUSEUM

The old quarry workshops at Gilfach Ddu now act as a museum of quarry machinery and associated relics. The building itself is rather strange in that it gives the appearance of being an old fort. The workshops housed in this large building include smithies, fitting shops, a saw mill, a carpenter's shop, a pattern shop, a foundry and locomotive repair works. These buildings, arranged round a central courtyard, were used to construct and repair the quarry machinery and thus make the quarry independent of outside assistance. All the machines were originally driven by line shafting from a single 80hp waterwheel, 50ft 5in in diameter and 5ft 3in wide. It was designed and manufactured by the de Winton works and installed at Gilfach Ddu in 1870 when the works complex was built. The water tank is 55ft above ground level. The wheel ran out of control twice during its working life but was soon repaired within a few hours. It ceased to be used after 1925 when it was replaced by a Pelton waterwheel. The de Winton wheel is now on public show.

The works foundry is dominated by a large hand-operated crane made entirely of wood and wooden patterns ranging from chairs to waggon wheels and machine gears are also on display. The cupola remains in the foundry; iron was melted in this before being poured into the existing moulds and all in all the foundry remains much as it was when in use.

Other than the workshops, smithy and dressing shed there still exists the works' hospital complete with beds, doctor's equipment and artificial limbs, the canteen where the men had their meals and sundry notices or rules and regulations to be upheld. The whole building abounds with relics that need little imagination to conjure up past activity. The slate blocks and the roofing slates used during the construction came—naturally—from the Dinorwic Quarry, whilst the iron frames for the windows were cast in the foundry. The complete works was built in 1870 and was used through to the closure of the quarry in 1969 when Caernarvonshire County Council agreed to take over the premises so that it could be protected by the Department of the Environment, under whose auspices the National Museum of Wales would establish a slate quarrying museum of North Wales. Primarily based on Dinorwic relics, it is intended to extend coverage to include items from other quarries as well.

The locomotive works housed in one corner of the premises are connected to the Llanberis Lake Railway, as mentioned above, and are used by that concern for their original purpose; inside the courtyard the Padarn Railway and the Dinorwic system are well represented by a variety of preserved items. Rolling stock includes a hand-cranked velocipede, an eight-seater incline carriage of early design, several slab, slate and rubbish waggons together with a crude platelayers' truck for use on the Padarn Railway. Trackwork is represented by a variety of rail types, a fixed point and two curious waggon turntables used in the works, still in situ, on which the waggons were turned on rail-less metal discs in order to gain access to the various shops.

### PRESERVED LOCOMOTIVES

The following list (believed to be correct at the time of writing) attempts to give details of those Padarn, Dinorwic and Penrhyn engines which have escaped the scrapman's torch. The locomotive's identity given is that carried at the time of disposal; any subsequent change is also recorded. Not all the locomotives are on view to the public; those that are are classified as either static or working exhibits. Finally, it should

## Ex-Padarn
  *Fire Queen:* Horlock /1848. Industrial Railway Museum, Penrhyn Castle, Bangor. Static.

## Ex-Dinorwic
  *Velinheli:* Hunslet 409/1886. Privately preserved.
  *King of the Scarlets:* Hunslet 492/1889. Privately preserved (Ontario, Canada).
  *Red Damsel:* Hunslet 493/1889. Llanberis Lake Railway. Working. Now named No 1 *Elidir* and fitted with a cab latterly off *Irish Mail.*
  *Rough Pup:* Hunslet 541/1891. Narrow Gauge Railway Museum, Towyn, Merioneth. Static.
  *Cloister:* Hunslet 542/1891. Hampshire Narrow Gauge Railway Society, Durley, Hants. Working. Note—it has been stated in the past that this engine is actually *Wild Aster* (Hunslet 849/1904) with false identity. It was however inspected and sold in 1962 as 542/1891 and during subsequent restoration work all major parts were found to be stamped 542; some minor parts bore other numbers (a result of the Dinorwic Quarry's policy of pooling spares) but *none* the number 849.
  *Jerry M:* Hunslet 638/1895. Hollycombe Woodland Garden, Steam Fair & Steam Railway, Liphook, Sussex. Working.
  *Cackler:* Hunslet 671/1898. Privately preserved.
  *Bernstein:* Hunslet 678/1898. Lytham Motive Power Museum, Lytham, Lancs. Working. Now No 10 *Jonathan.*
  *Covertcoat:* Hunslet 679/1898. Privately preserved.
  *George B:* Hunslet 680/1898. Dowty Railway Preservation Society, Aschurch, Glos. Working.
  *Holy War:* Hunslet 779/1902. Quainton Railway Society, Quainton Road Station, Bucks. Working.
  *Alice:* Hunslet 780/1902. West Lancashire Light Railway, Hesketh Bank, near Southport, Lancs. Now being restored to working order—a rather formidable task (see Chapter 5)!

*Maid Marian:* Hunslet 822/1903. Llanberis Lake Railway. Working.

*Irish Mail:* Hunslet 823/1903. West Lancashire Light Railway. Undergoing a rebuild to an 0-4-2 saddle tank to accommodate a larger boiler. To be No 3 *Irish Mail.*

*Wild Aster:* Hunslet 849/1904. Llanberis Lake Railway. Working. Now No 2 *Wild Aster* and fitted with a spare cab.

*Sybil:* Bagnall 1760/1906. Privately preserved.

*No 1:* Hunslet 1429/1922. Knebworth West Park & Wintergreen Railway, Knebworth, Herts. Working.

*Dolbadarn:* Hunslet 1430/1922. Llanberis Lake Railway. Working. The Alice class boiler has been removed and a domed one fitted. The cab has been replaced.

*No 70:* Barclay 1995/1931. Hollycombe Woodland Garden, Steam Fair & Steam Railway. Working. Now named *Caledonia.*

*Michael:* Hunslet 1709/1932. Privately preserved (Ontario).

*Elidir:* Avonside 2071/1933. Privately preserved (Canada).

*D1:* Ruston & Hornsby 277265/1949. Llanberis Lake Railway. Working. Now No 4 *Chwarelwr.*

Ex-Penrhyn

*Kathleen:* de Winton /1877. Privately preserved.

*George Henry:* de Winton /1877. Narrow Gauge Railway Museum, Towyn. Static.

*Charles:* Hunslet 283/1883. Industrial Railway Museum, Penrhyn Castle. Static.

*Gwynedd:* Hunslet 316/1883. Bressingham Steam Museum, Diss, Norfolk. Working.

*Lillian:* Hunslet 317/1883. Privately preserved.

*Winifred:* Hunslet 364/1885. Early Wheels Museum, Terre Haute, Indiana, USA. Static.

*Lilla:* Hunslet 554/1891. Privately preserved.

*Blanche:* Hunslet 589/1893. Festiniog Railway. Working. Since its acquisition by the FR *Blanche* has been converted to a 2-4-0 tender locomotive, fitted with a superheater and is now oil-fired.

*Linda:* Hunslet 590/1893. Ffestiniog Railway. Working. Rebuilt as per *Blanche.*

*Margaret:* Hunslet 605/1894. Cadeby Light Railway, Leics. Working.

*Alan George:* Hunslet 606/1894. Howdenclough Light Railway, Bruntcliffe, Leeds. Working.

*Jubilee 1897:* Manning, Wardle 1382/1897. Narrow Gauge Railway Museum, Towyn. Static.

*Nesta:* Hunslet 704/1899. Privately preserved (USA).

*Elin:* Hunslet 705/1899. Lincolnshire Coast Light Railway. Working.

*Hugh Napier:* Hunslet 855/1904. Industrial Railway Museum, Penrhyn Castle. Static.

*Pamela:* Hunslet 920/1906. Privately preserved.

*Sybil Mary:* Hunslet 921/1906. Privately preserved.

*George Sholto:* Hunslet 994/1909. Bressingham Steam Museum. Working.

*Gertrude:* Hunslet 995/1909. Ontario Science Centre, Toronto, Canada. Has been beautifully sectioned for display.

*Edward Sholto:* Hunslet 996/1909. Privately preserved (Ontario).

*Eigiau:* Orenstein & Koppel 5668/1912. Bressingham Steam Museum. Working. Now also carries the number 1.

*No 2 Felin Hen:* Baldwin 46828/1917. Bundaberg Lions Park, Queensland, Australia. Static. In later 0-6-2 tank form, complete with spark arrester.

*Stanhope:* Kerr, Stuart 2395/1917. Bressingham Steam Museum. This locomotive is not strictly speaking preserved for most parts have been removed (see Chapter 5); in 1969 the boiler was utilised for the rebuilding of *Bronllwyd* (see below).

*Sgt. Murphy:* Kerr, Stuart 3117/1918. Cadeby Light Railway. Working.

*Bronllwyd:* Hudswell, Clarke 1643/1930. Bressingham Steam Museum. Working. The remains of this locomotive were rebuilt in 1969 with the boiler from *Stanhope* and it is now running in its new, cabless guise.

*Cegin:* Barclay 1991/1931. Privately preserved, USA.

*Glyder:* Barclay 1994/1931. Privately preserved, USA.

*Ogwen:* Avonside 2066/1933. Privately preserved, USA.

*Marchlyn:* Avonside 2067/1933. Lake Winnepasuka Amusement Park, Rossville, Georgia, USA.
22: Ruston & Hornsby 226302/1944. Privately preserved.
24: Ruston & Hornsby 382820/1955. Privately preserved.

OTHER PRESERVED ITEMS

An excellent collection of preserved Penrhyn relics, apart from the locomotives referred to above, can be seen at Penrhyn Castle. The Penrhyn Railway exhibits include Lord Penrhyn's private saloon, a quarrymen's carriage, coal waggon No 1A, fullersite waggon No 77, slate waggon No 230 and two bolster waggons. There is also an incline carriage, two rubbish waggons (one with early wood frames and one with later steel frames) and a slab waggon, all originally used in the quarry. A major exhibit is a length of track made up from the different types of rail used in the quarry, ranging from the heaviest section down to the lightest, each complete with its appropriate type of points (see Chapter 2). Also on show is a collection of original name plates from Penrhyn locomotives, a model of the Penrhyn Railway and a slate industry display.

Among other industrial railway exhibits at the museum are several Padarn and Dinorwic items. These comprise, in addition to *Fire Queen*, Assheton-Smith's private carriage, the hand-cranked velocipede *Arthur*, a foot-operated velocipede, a one-man velocipede with wire spoke wheels converted from an old bicycle and a six-seater incline carriage.

Other preserved items, apart from those in private collections and those at the Gilfach Ddu museum already described, include Padarn transporter No 70, complete with three slate waggons and a guard's van, a selection of Padarn and Dinorwic track material, a Penrhyn Railway signal and a collection of locomotive name and works plates at the Narrow Gauge Railway Museum at Towyn; Dinorwic slate waggon No 623 at the Albany Steam and Industrial Museum, Isle of Wight; and Dinorwic slab waggon No 15 at the Brockham Narrow Gauge and Industrial Railway Museum, Surrey.

## TRAMROADS, RAILWAYS AND PORTS

Virtually nothing immediately apparent exists of the original Penrhyn and Dinorwic tramroads. Time has taken its toll and much of the routes has been farmed over, built on or completely obliterated by new roads. Now and again a faint glimpse of the old trackbeds can be seen, indicated by the odd stretch of embankment, incline or footpath. Some of the stone sleepers remain half-buried along the way.

The first stretch of the Padarn Railway is today occupied by the Llanberis Lake Railway, as described above; from Penllyn to Penscoins the route can easily be followed although in several places it is overgrown. Still the characteristic stone walls on either side chart its progress. All the underline bridges have been removed but all the overbridges remain, including the unique footbridge at Bethel. The brick crossing keepers' huts, the stone platforms, carriage and locomotive sheds still stand, though in a very decrepit state. A similar situation exists on the Penrhyn and although it is far more overgrown it too remains traceable. Again all track and fittings have been removed, leaving but some rotting sleepers in places.

The incline down to Port Dinorwic is still easily visible beneath the undergrowth. Some changes have been made—the bridge over the Bangor-Caernarvon railway has been dismantled along with the minor road bridge immediately above it—but the tunnel beneath the main road still exists. All the track in the port has been lifted but many of the various port buildings still stand. Since its 'closure' (it is actually occasionally still used for cargo boats) the port has been acquired by a private concern for redevelopment, under the name Raybourne Marina, as a luxury mooring for yachts and cruisers. New buildings have been erected and 'landscaping' is in the process of being gradually carried out. By the dry dock (still very much in service) there still stands lot 611 left over from the 1969 auction, a 1904 Smith Rodley self-propelled steam crane, No 6618. Running along the dock edge on 7ft gauge track, this meant that the port was in the interesting—if not unique—position of having narrow, standard and broad gauge trackwork all in use at the same time!

Again a similar situation exists at Port Penrhyn with several buildings left standing as an indication of its former use. Part of the quayside is used for the dumping (before removal by lorry) of sand dredged from the Menai Straits. It is no longer used as a port, except for the occasional mooring of the local mussel boats, but a plan has been proposed to develop the port, including the whole of the Bangor sea front, as another, even larger, marina. Part of the premises has recently (1973) been converted into a fish-processing plant; the former slate works is now in use as a foundry.

# Appendices

## APPENDIX I
## CHRONOLOGY

### PADARN

- 1787 Thomas Assheton-Smith lets the largest Dinorwic quarry to the Dinorwic Slate Co.
- 1793 Assheton-Smith enlarges quay at Y Felinheli, renamed Port Dinorwic.
- 1799 Gallery system adopted at Dinorwic.
- 1809 Assheton-Smith forms Dinorwic Quarry Co.
- 1816 First quarry tramroads built.
- 1824 Dinorwic Tramroad built.
- 1841 June. Padarn Railway begun.
- 1843 December. Padarn Railway completed and working (horse traction). Dinorwic Tramroad abandoned.
- 1848 Steam locomotives introduced on the Padarn Railway.
- 1852 Bangor & Caernarvon Railway reaches Port Dinorwic.
- 1856 B & CR constructs siding down to quay at Port Dinorwic.
- 1869 1 July. LNWR branch to Llanberis opened.

### PENRHYN

- 1768 21 year leases introduced for slate workings.
- 1782 Richard Pennant buys out leases and runs the workings himself.
- 1790 Pennant builds Port Penrhyn.
- 1798 Greenfield invents gallery system of working. First quarry tramroads built.
- 1800 October. Penrhyn Tramroad begun.
- 1801 June. Penrhyn Tramroad completed.
- 1820 Group of quarrymen found Bethesda.
- 1852 Port Penrhyn branch opened by Chester & Holyhead Railway.

| PADARN | PENRHYN |
|---|---|
| 1870 Steam traction introduced at Dinorwic. | |
| | 1876 Steam locomotive used on top section of Penrhyn Tramroad. Steam traction introduced in the quarry. |
| | 1878 Penrhyn Railway built. Tramroad abandoned. |
| | 1879 2 February. Workmen's passenger service commences. |
| | 1882 Lord Penrhyn's private saloon constructed. |
| | 1884 1 July. LNWR Bethesda branch opened. |
| 1895 Workmen's passenger service commences. | |
| 1896 Assheton-Smith's private saloon constructed. | |
| 1924 May. Port incline converted from continuous chain to self-acting cable. | |
| 1926 22 January. Fatal accident with oil lorry on Padarn Railway. | 1932 Internal combustion locomotives introduced at Penrhyn. |
| 1935 Internal combustion locomotives introduced at Dinorwic. | |
| 1947 8 November. Workmen's service ceases. | 1951 9 February. Workmen's service ceases. |
| 1954 Major rockfall at Dinorwic. | 1954 Port Penrhyn branch reduced to siding status. |
| 1961 27 October. Last working run over Padarn Railway. 30 October. Port Dinorwic siding closes. | |
| 1962 7 September. Llanberis branch closes. | 1962 24 July. Penrhyn Railway closes. |

## PADARN

1963 Lifting of Padarn Railway completed.

1967 Steam working ceases at Dinorwic.
1969 July. Last 350 workers laid off at Dinorwic.
12 & 13 December. Quarry equipment auctioned.
1970 23 June. Quarry auctioned.
1971 28 May. Llanberis Lake Railway inaugurated.

## PENRHYN

1963 2 March. Port Penrhyn branch closes.
6 October. Bethesda branch closes.
1964 Last year of steam working at Penrhyn.
1965 25 June. Industrial Railway Museum opens at Penrhyn Castle. Penrhyn Railway lifted.

## APPENDIX 2
## PADARN RAILWAY LOCOMOTIVE STOCK LIST

| Name | Builder | Works No | Date | Type | Remarks |
|---|---|---|---|---|---|
| Fire Queen | Horlock | — | 1848 | 0-4-0; | withdrawn c1882; preserved |
| Jenny Lind | Horlock | — | 1848 | 0-4-0; | scrapped c1886 |
| Dinorwic | Hunslet | 302 | 1882 | 0-6-0T; | scrapped 1963 |
| Amalthaea | Hunslet | 410 | 1886 | 0-6-0T; | Pandora till 1909; scrapped 1963 |
| Velinheli | Hunslet | 631 | 1895 | 0-6-0T; | dismantled for repairs 1953, never reassembled; scrapped 1963 |
| — | Hardy | 954 | 1925 | | 4w petrol-mechanical; scrapped 1963 |

*All built to order*

## APPENDIX 3
## PADARN RAILWAY STEAM: COMPARATIVE DIMENSIONS

| | Horlock 0-4-0s | Hunslet 0-6-0Ts |
|---|---|---|
| Wheel diameter | 4ft 6in | 3ft 6in |
| Wheelbase (total) | 12ft 0½in | 10ft 0in |
| Cylinders: diameter | 13in | 12½in |
| : stroke | 22in | 20in |
| Boiler: diameter | 3ft 0in | 3ft 4½in |
| : length | 8ft 3½in | 8ft 0in |
| : no of tubes | 86 | 119 |
| : working pressure | 60lb/sq in | 140lb/sq in |
| Heating surface: tubes | 386.3sq ft | 458.0sq ft |
| : firebox | 50.5sq ft | 49.0sq ft |
| : total | 436.8sq ft | 507.0sq ft |
| Grate area | 9.75sq ft | 8.0sq ft |
| Water capacity | * | 600gal |
| Fuel capacity | * | 1 ton |
| Weight: empty | * | 21tons 14cwt |
| : in working order | * | 26tons 0cwt |
| Overall dimensions: length | 33ft 10in | * |
| : width | * | 7ft 10¼in |
| : height | 11ft 6in | 11ft 8¼in |
| Tractive effort at 75% | 3098lb | 7812lb |

*figures not available

## APPENDIX 4

### DINORWIC STEAM STOCK LIST

| Name | Builder | Works No | Date | Type | Remarks |
|---|---|---|---|---|---|
| Wellington | de Winton | — | c1870 | 0-4-0VBT | Sold by 1900 |
| Harriet | de Winton | — | c1870 | 0-4-0VBT | |
| Peris | de Winton | — | c1870 | 0-4-0VBT | Single Cylinder; details unknown |
| Victoria | de Winton | — | c1870 | 0-4-0VBT | |
| Charlie | Hunslet | 51 | 1870 | 0-4-0ST | Originally Dinorwic; withdrawn 1916; scrapped c1940 |
| George | Hunslet | 184 | 1877 | 0-4-0ST | Withdrawn 1916; sold 1919 |
| Louisa | Hunslet | 195 | 1877 | 0-4-0ST | Sold c1898 |
| Velinheli | Hunslet | 409 | 1886 | 0-4-0ST | Preserved |
| King of the Scarlets | Hunslet | 492 | 1889 | 0-4-0ST | Originally *Alice*; preserved |
| Red Damsel | Hunslet | 493 | 1889 | 0-4-0ST | Originally *Enid*; preserved |
| Rough Pup | Hunslet | 541 | 1891 | 0-4-0ST | Originally No 1; preserved |
| Cloister | Hunslet | 542 | 1891 | 0-4-0ST | Originally No 2; preserved |
| Jerry M | Hunslet | 638 | 1895 | 0-4-0ST | Originally *Vaenol*; preserved |
| Lady Madcap | Hunslet | 652 | 1896 | 0-4-0ST | Originally *Elidir* at Dinorwic; purchased 1910; scrapped 1952 |
| Cackler | Hunslet | 671 | 1898 | 0-4-0ST | Originally *Port Dinorwic*; preserved |
| Bernstein | Hunslet | 678 | 1898 | 0-4-0ST | Originally *The First*; preserved |
| Covertcoat | Hunslet | 679 | 1898 | 0-4-0ST | Originally *The Second*; preserved |

L

178　THE PADARN AND PENRHYN RAILWAYS

| Name | Builder | Works No | Date | Type | Remarks |
|---|---|---|---|---|---|
| George B | Hunslet | 680 | 1898 | 0-4-0ST | Originally *Wellington*; preserved |
| Holy War | Hunslet | 779 | 1902 | 0-4-0ST | Originally No 3; preserved |
| Alice | Hunslet | 780 | 1902 | 0-4-0ST | Originally No 4; preserved |
| Maid Marian | Hunslet | 822 | 1903 | 0-4-0ST | Originally No 5; preserved |
| Irish Mail | Hunslet | 823 | 1903 | 0-4-0ST | Originally No 6; preserved |
| Wild Aster | Hunslet | 849 | 1904 | 0-4-0ST | Originally No 7; preserved |
| Sybil | Bagnall | 1760 | 1906 | 0-4-0ST | Preserved |
| No 1 | Hunslet | 1429 | 1922 | 0-4-0ST | One-time *Lady Joan*; preserved |
| Dolbadarn | Hunslet | 1430 | 1922 | 0-4-0ST | Originally No 2; preserved |
| No 70 | Barclay | 1995 | 1931 | 0-4-0WT | Purchased 1948; preserved |
| Michael | Hunslet | 1709 | 1932 | 0-4-0ST | Preserved |
| Elidir | Avonside | 2071 | 1933 | 0-4-0T | Purchased 1949; preserved |

VBT — vertical-boilered tank engine
ST — saddle tank engine
WT — well tank engine
T — side tank engine

APPENDIX 5

## DINORWIC HUNSLETS: COMPARATIVE DIMENSIONS

|  | Alice & Port classes | Mills class |
|---|---|---|
| Wheel diameter | 1ft 8in | 2ft 2in |
| Wheelbase | 3ft 3in | 4ft 6in |
| Cylinders: diameter | 7in | 8½in |
| : stroke | 10in | 14in |
| Boiler: diameter | 1ft 11¾in | 2ft 3in |
| : length | 6ft 0in | 8ft 0in |
| : no of tubes | 28 | 45 |
| : working pressure | 140lb/sq in (160) | 140lb/sq in |
| Heating surface: tubes | 86sq ft | 171sq ft |
| : firebox | 14sq ft | 22sq ft |
| : total | 100sq ft | 193sq ft |
| Grate area | 2.5sq ft | 3.5sq ft |
| Water capacity | 100gal | 220gal |
| Fuel capacity | 1½cwt | 3cwt |
| Weight: empty | 5t 10cwt (5t 19cwt) | 10t 0cwt |
| : in working order | 6t 0cwt (6t 14cwt) | 11t 15cwt |
| Overall dimensions: length | 13ft 0in | 17ft 5¼in |
| : width | 5ft 4in | 6ft 0in |
| : height | 7ft 3in (8ft 3in) | 7ft 10in |
| Tractive effort at 75% | 2578lb (2940lb) | 4085lb |

*All 0-4-0ST design*

*Dimensions in brackets are for Port classes (with cabs)*

*NB — all dimensions subject to individual variations owing to wear, tear and general repairs*

APPENDIX 6

## DINORWIC INTERNAL COMBUSTION STOCK LIST

| No | Builder | Works No | Date | Type | Second-hand Arrival |
|---|---|---|---|---|---|
| A2 | R & H | 175987 | 1935 | Diesel | — |
| A1 | R & H | 181807 | 1936 | Diesel | — |
| E3 | R & H | 186322 | 1937 | Diesel | 1950 |
| E4 | R & H | 186342 | 1937 | Diesel | 1950 |
| E6 | R & H | 191645 | 1938 | Diesel | 1950* |
| E5 | R & H | 191661 | 1938 | Diesel | 1950 |
| E10 | R & H | 202979 | 1940 | Diesel | 1956 |
| E8 | R & H | 203009 | 1941 | Diesel | 1952 |
| E1 | R & H | 211598 | 1941 | Diesel | 1947 |
| E2 | R & H | 211620 | 1941 | Diesel | 1947* |
| E7 | R & H | 221605 | 1943 | Diesel | 1952 |
| E11 | R & H | 222081 | 1943 | Diesel | 1957 |
| E9 | R & H | 235704 | 1945 | Diesel | 1956 |
| C1 | Hibberd | 2782 | 1945 | Diesel | — |
| C3 | Hibberd | 2791 | 1945 | Diesel | — |
| C2 | Hibberd | 2792 | 1945 | Diesel | — |
| — | Lister | 28068 | 1946 | Petrol | — |
| B2 | R & H | 246809 | 1947 | Diesel | — |
| B1 | R & H | 252799 | 1947 | Diesel | — |
| D2 | R & H | 273854 | 1949 | Diesel | — |
| D1 | R & H | 277265 | 1949 | Diesel | —** |
| D3 | R & H | 277269 | 1949 | Diesel | — |

R & H: *Ruston and Hornsby*

*All 4-wheeled, mechanical transmission*

*All withdrawn and cannibalised or scrapped by 1969 except:*
  *\*Still surviving in quarry*
  *\*\*Preserved on Llanberis Lake Railway as No 4*

*Numbers are those originally allocated*

APPENDICES 181

APPENDIX 7

## PENRHYN RAILWAY LOCOMOTIVE STOCK LIST

| Name | Builder | Works No | Date | Remarks |
|---|---|---|---|---|
| Edward Sholto | de Winton | — | 1878 | 0-4-0ST; scrapped 1907 |
| Hilda | de Winton | — | 1878 | 0-4-0T; scrapped post-1911 |
| Violet | de Winton | — | 1878 | 0-4-0T; scrapped 1902 |
| Charles | Hunslet | 283 | 1882 | 0-4-0ST; withdrawn 1962; preserved |
| Blanche | Hunslet | 589 | 1893 | 0-4-0ST; withdrawn 1962; preserved |
| Linda | Hunslet | 590 | 1893 | 0-4-0ST; withdrawn 1962; preserved |
| No 1 Llandegai | Baldwin | 47143 | 1917 | 2-6-2T; acquired 1923; withdrawn 1927; scrapped 1940 |
| No 2 Felin Hen | Baldwin | 46828 | 1917 | 2-6-2T; acquired 1923; withdrawn 1927; sold 1940; preserved |
| No 3 Tregarth | Baldwin | 46764 | 1917 | 2-6-2T; acquired 1923; withdrawn 1928; scrapped 1940 |

APPENDIX 8

PENRHYN (PORT & QUARRY) STEAM STOCK LIST

| Name | Builder | Works No | Date | Type | Remarks |
|---|---|---|---|---|---|
| George Sholto | Hughes? | — | c1876 | 0-4-0T | Used on first section of Penrhyn Tramroad; fate unknown |
| Lord Penrhyn | de Winton | — | 1876 | 0-4-0VBT | Scrapped 1909 |
| Lady Penrhyn | de Winton | — | 1876 | 0-4-0VBT | Scrapped after 1911 |
| Alice | de Winton | — | 1876 | 0-4-0VBT | Scrapped after 1911 |
| Georgina | de Winton | — | 1877 | 0-4-0VBT | Scrapped 1904 |
| Ina | de Winton | — | 1877 | 0-4-0VBT | Scrapped 1911 |
| Kathleen | de Winton | — | 1877 | 0-4-0VBT | Withdrawn 1911; dismantled 1939; preserved |
| George Henry | de Winton | — | 1877 | 0-4-0VBT | Withdrawn 1911; preserved |
| Bronllwyd | Hughes? | — | c1878 | 0-4-0VBT | Believed to have been Coetmor used on construction of Penrhyn Railway; converted to stationary engine; scrapped 1906 |
| Gwynedd | Hunslet | 316 | 1883 | 0-4-0ST | Preserved |
| Lilian | Hunslet | 317 | 1883 | 0-4-0ST | Preserved |
| Winifred | Hunslet | 364 | 1885 | 0-4-0ST | Preserved |
| Lilla | Hunslet | 554 | 1891 | 0-4-0ST | Purchased 1928; preserved |
| Margaret | Hunslet | 605 | 1894 | 0-4-0ST | Preserved |
| Alan George | Hunslet | 606 | 1894 | 0-4-0ST | Preserved |

APPENDICES 183

| Name | Builder | Works No | Date | Type | Remarks |
|---|---|---|---|---|---|
| Jubilee 1897 | MW | 1382 | 1897 | 0-4-0ST | Purchased 1928; preserved |
| Nesta | Hunslet | 704 | 1899 | 0-4-0ST | Preserved |
| Elin | Hunslet | 705 | 1899 | 0-4-0ST | Preserved |
| Sanford | Bagnall | 1571 | 1900 | 0-4-0ST | Purchased 1929; converted to brake van 1956 |
| Hugh Napier | Hunslet | 855 | 1904 | 0-4-0ST | Preserved |
| Skinner | Bagnall | 1766 | 1906 | 0-4-0ST | Purchased 1929; dismantled 1954 |
| Pamela | Hunslet | 920 | 1906 | 0-4-0ST | Preserved |
| Sybil Mary | Hunslet | 921 | 1906 | 0-4-0ST | Preserved |
| George Sholto | Hunslet | 994 | 1909 | 0-4-0ST | Preserved |
| Gertrude Edward | Hunslet | 995 | 1909 | 0-4-0ST | Preserved |
| Sholto | Hunslet | 996 | 1909 | 0-4-0ST | Preserved |
| Eigiau | O & K | 5668 | 1912 | 0-4-0WT | Purchased 1929; preserved |
| Stanhope | KS | 2395 | 1917 | 0-4-2ST | Purchased 1934; withdrawn 1947; parts disposed of |
| Sgt. Murphy | KS | 3117 | 1918 | 0-6-0T | Purchased 1922; rebuilt 1932; preserved |
| Bronllwyd | HC | 1643 | 1930 | 0-6-0WT | Purchased 1934; named 1937; preserved |
| Cegin | Barclay | 1991 | 1931 | 0-4-0WT | Purchased 1936; preserved |
| Glyder | Barclay | 1994 | 1931 | 0-4-0WT | Purchased 1938; preserved |
| Ogwen | Avonside | 2066 | 1933 | 0-4-0T | Purchased 1936; preserved |
| Marchlyn | Avonside | 2067 | 1933 | 0-4-0T | Purchased 1936; preserved |

MW — Manning, Wardle  
O & K — Orenstein & Koppel  
KS — Kerr, Stuart  
HC — Hudswell, Clarke  

T — side tank engine  
VBT — vertical-boilered tank engine  
ST — saddle tank engine  
WT — well tank engine

## APPENDIX 9

### PENRHYN HUNSLETS: COMPARATIVE DIMENSIONS

|  | Main line class | Port class | Small class | Large class |
|---|---|---|---|---|
| Wheel diameter | 2ft 1in | 1ft 8in | 1ft 8in | 1ft 8in |
| Wheelbase | 5ft 0in | 4ft 0in | 3ft 3in | 4ft 0in |
| Cylinders: diameter | 10½in* | 7in | 7in | 7½in |
| : stroke | 12in | 10in | 10in | 10in |
| Working pressure, lb/sq in | 140 | 120 | 120 | 140 |
| Water capacity | 270gal | 150gal | 100gal | 150gal |
| Fuel capacity | 5.5cwt | 2cwt | 1.5cwt | 2cwt |
| Weight in working order | 12t 6cwt* | 7t 10cwt | 6t 0cwt | 7t 12cwt |
| Overall dimensions: length | 18ft 6in | 13ft 10in | 13ft 0in | 13ft 10in |
| : width | 5ft 8in | 5ft 4in | 5ft 4in | 5ft 4in |
| : height | 8ft 0in | 7ft 8in | 7ft 3in | 7ft 8in |
| Tractive effort at 75% | 5557lb* | 2205lb | 2205lb | 2953lb |

All 0-4-0ST design

*Charles (283): 10in diameter cylinders
: 12t 5cwt in working order
: 5040lb tractive effort

NB — all dimensions subject to individual variatians owing to wear, tear and general repairs

## APPENDIX 10

### PENRHYN INTERNAL COMBUSTION STOCK LIST

| No | Builder | Date | Remarks |
|---|---|---|---|
| *Petrol* | | | |
| 1–18 | PQ | 1932-9 | Fitted with Morris car engines. No 1 rebuilt with Lister diesel engine 1946; others withdrawn and scrapped later |

| No | Builder | Works No | Date Built | Date Purchased | Remarks |
|---|---|---|---|---|---|
| *Diesel* | | | | | |
| 1 | PQ | — | 1932 | — | Ex-No 1 from Petrol list |
| 2 | R & H | 198292 | 1940 | 1946 | |
| 3 | R & H | 218033 | 1943 | 1947 | |
| 4 | R & H | 218011 | 1943 | 1947 | |
| 5 | R & H | 222072 | 1943 | 1947 | |
| 6 | R & H | 223674 | 1943 | 1947 | |
| 7 | R & H | 223680 | 1943 | 1947 | |
| 8 | R & H | 187084 | 1937 | 1948 | |
| 9 | R & H | 183763 | 1937 | 1948 | |
| 10 | R & H | 181818 | 1936 | 1948 | |
| 11 | R & H | 189994 | 1938 | 1948 | |
| 12 | R & H | 181812 | 1936 | 1948 | |
| 13 | R & H | 211596 | 1941 | 1949 | |
| 14 | R & H | 211605 | 1941 | 1949 | |
| 15 | R & H | 202976 | 1940 | 1949 | |
| 16 | R & H | 211640 | 1941 | 1949 | |
| 17 | PQ | — | c1950 | — | R & H engine in ex-petrol locomotive frame |
| 18 | R & H | 223685 | 1944 | 1951 | |
| 19 | R & H | 223701 | 1944 | 1951 | |
| 20 | R & H | 223753 | 1944 | 1951 | |
| 21 | R & H | 226297 | 1944 | 1951 | |
| 22 | R & H | 226302 | 1944 | 1951 | Preserved |
| 23 | R & H | 229651 | 1944 | 1951 | |
| 24 | R & H | 382820 | 1955 | 1955 | Preserved |

PQ – Penrhyn Quarry

*R & H: Ruston & Hornsby*
*All 4w mechanical transmission*
*All scrapped before or at closure of rail system unless otherwise noted*

# Bibliography

## BACKGROUND WORKS
Assheton-Smith, C. G. *Dinorwic Slate Quarries.* (North Wales, undated)
Carr, H. R. & Lister, G. A. (ed). *The Mountains of Snowdonia.* (2nd ed. 1948)
Davies, D. C. *Treatise on Slates and Slate Quarrying.* (1878)
Dodd, A. H. *A History of Caernarvonshire.* (Caernarvon, 1968). *The Industrial Revolution in North Wales.* (Cardiff, 2nd ed. 1972)
Eardley-Wilmot, Sir J. *Thomas Assheton-Smith.* (1859)
Evans, Rev. J. *Topographical and Historical Description of the Counties of Caernarvon and Denbigh.* (1810)
Lewis, Samuel. *Topographical Dictionary of Wales.* Vol II (1838)
Maxwell, Sir Herbert. *Reminiscences of the late Thomas Assheton-Smith Esq.* (Essex, 1859)
North, F. J. *The Slates of Wales.* (Cardiff, 1925)
Pritchard, D. Dylan. *The Slate Industry of North Wales.* (1946)

## RAILWAY WORKS
Bradley, V. J. & Hindley, P. H. *Industrial and Independent Railways in North Wales.* (1968)
Jones, R. B. *British Narrow Gauge Railways.* (1958)
Lee, C. E. *Narrow-Gauge Railways in North Wales.* (1945) *The Penrhyn Railway.* (1972)
Tredgold, T. *A Practical Treatise on Rail-Roads and Carriages.* (1825)
*Llanberis Lake Railway*

## PERIODICALS
*Caernarvon Record Office Bulletin*
*Locomotive Magazine*
*Mining Journal*
*Model Railway News*
*Modern Tramway*
*Narrow Gauge Illustrated*
*Quarry Manager's Journal*
*Railway Magazine*
*Railway World*

## NEWSPAPERS

*Caernarvon & Denbigh Herald*
*North Wales Chronicle*
*North Wales Gazette*
*The (Manchester) Guardian*
*The Times*
Other local and national newspapers

## OTHER SOURCES

*Industrial Railway Museum Penrhyn Castle* (guide book)
*North Wales Quarrying Museum Dinorwic* (guide book)
*Penny Cyclopaedia. Vol XIX.* (1841)
*Repertory of Arts and Manufactures. Vol III.* (Second series, 1803)
OS maps: 1in and 25in
Act of Parliament: 7 & 8 Vic c65
Manuscripts: Caernarvon Record Office Penrhyn Quarry and Dinorwic Quarry collections

# Index

For subjects relating to the Padarn Railway; Penrhyn Railway, Quarry and Tramroad; Dinorwic Quarry and Tramroad; Port Penrhyn and Port Dinorwic, refer to the Contents and List of Illustrations pages. Plate numbers are given in italic type.

Abercegin, 16, 54
Aberogwen, 13, 16
Accidents, 74, 119, 121, 131–5, 174
Acts of Parliament, 20, 45, 89
Afon Cegin, 13, 14, 16, 40, 41, 43, 54, 57
Afon Ogwen, 13, 14, 39, 41, 43, 53
Afon Rhythallt, 74
Afon Saint, 74
Albany Steam & Industrial Museum, 170
Algeo, Mr, 48
Allt Dhu workings, 65, 152
Anglesea gallery, 155
Anglesey, 16, 54, 119, 164
Anglesey Shipping Co, 56
Assheton-Smith, C. G. D., 35; C. M. R. V. D., 93; E., 81; G. W. D., 77, 82, 120, 121, 131, 174; T. (elder), 18, 67, 84, 173; T. (younger), 18–22, 67–72, 76, 84
Auctions, 96–8, 156, 175
Australia, 92, 102, 169
Australia gallery, 152
Avonside Engine Co, 113, 155; locomotives, 113, 155–6, 169, 170, 178, 183

Bagnall, W. G. Ltd, 110, 155; locomotives, 110, 155, 168, 178, 183
Baldwin Locomotive Works, 101; locomotives, 62, 101–2, 108, 109, 169, 181
Bangor, 13ff, 40ff, 54, 57, 58, 63, 65, 68, 81, 86, 89, 98, 167, 171, 172; Bishop of, 16
Bangor & Caernarvon Rly, 84, 89, 173
Barclay, Andrew Sons & Co, 155; locomotives, 114, 155, 168, 169, 178, 183
Beatson, J., 108
Bethel, 74, 116, 121, 125, 127, 129, 131ff, 171; footbridge, 51, 74, 171

Bethesda, 41, 44, 48, 49, 53, 54, 61, 63, 110, 173, 174
Bethesda Junction, 58, 63
Bradley, V. J., 163
Bressingham Steam Museum, 152, 164, 168, 169
Brickworks, 35, 96
Broad gauge, 171–2
Brockham Narrow Gauge & Industrial Railway Museum, 170

Cadeby Light Rly, 169
Caernarvon, 11, 15ff, 41, 49, 61, 68, 74, 76, 81ff, 98, 99, 132, 135, 171
Caernarvonshire County Council, 98, 166
California gallery, 81
Canada, 107, 149, 150, 167ff
Capel Curig, 17
Carreg y Gwalch, see Penscoins
Carts, 16, 17, 23, 24, 40, 42, 131; see also Road transport
Cei Llydan, 164
Ceir gwylltion, 144; see also Velocipedes
Chester, 54, 57
Chester & Holyhead Rly, 45, 56, 57, 84, 89, 173
Cilgeraint incline, 41, 49, 108
Cilgwyn, 14, 110
Coed y Parc, 41, 49 59, 124
Commonland, 16, 18, 19, 20
Conway Valley, 11
Corris Rly, 113
Crampton, T. R., 135
Crauria Slate Works, 133, 134
Crown, the, 14, 16, 44

Dawkins-Pennant, G. H., 22, 44, 45
Deiniolen, 65, 119; inclines, 34, 65
De Winton & Co, 49, 97, 99, 102, 115, 135, 165; locomotives, 49, 61, 99–100, 102–3, 104, 107ff, 153, 154, 168, 177, 181, 182
Dinas incline, 31, 41, 53, 99

189

190 THE PADARN AND PENRHYN RAILWAYS

Dinorwic, 65, 119; Crown Manor, 18
Dinorwic Quarries Union, 77
Dinorwic Quarry Co, 20–22, 173
Dinorwic Quarry Museum, 35
Dinorwic Quarry Rly, 72
Dinorwic Slate Co, 18, 27, 173
Dinorwic Slate Quarries Co, 96
Diphwys gallery, 82
Dorothea Slate Quarry Co, 93
Douglas-Pennant, E. G. (1st Lord Penrhyn), 45, 46, 48, 61, 67; E. S. (3rd Lord Penrhyn), 62; G. S. G. (2nd Lord Penrhyn), 61, 62; H. N. (4th Lord Penrhyn), 62, 63
Dowty Railway Preservation Soc, 167
Dry dock, 91, 171
Dyffryn gallery, 149, 150

Elidir Fawr, 13, 18, 72
Enclosures, 20

Felinheli, Y, 18, 19, 24, 173
Felin Hen, 53, 54
Festiniog Rly, 47, 48, 63, 101, 149, 168
Ffestiniog, 43
Ffestiniog Slate Co, 22
Foulke, W., 71
France, 56, 62, 101
Fullersite, 59, 117, 170

Garret gallery, 38, 82
Germany, 84, 85, 92
Gilfach Dhu, 72, 79, 81, 87, 88, 95, 97, 125, 128, 129, 132, 138, 140, 143, 146, 148, 153, 155, 159, 162, 164, 165, 170
Glanybala, 71, 80
Gloucester Railway Carriage & Wagon Co, 125, 139–40
Glynrhonwy Slate Quarry Co, 153, 154
Glyn Valley Tramway, 101
Great Western Rly, 48
Greenfield, J., 24, 30, 173
Guards' van, 52, 158, 170

Halfway, 41, 42
Hampshire Narrow Gauge Railway Soc, 167
Hardy Motors Ltd, 138; locomotive, 70, 138–9, 176

Hendurnpike, 49, 54
Hibberd locomotives, 180
Holland, S., 43
Hollycombe Steam Fair & Steam Rly, 167, 168
Holyhead, 17, 54, 108
Horses, racing, 35, 146; working, 23, 39, 41, 42, 68, 131, 132, 143, 173; see also Road transport
Howdenclough Light Rly, 169
Hudswell, Clarke & Co, 112; locomotive, 112, 169, 183
Hughes, (Holyhead), 108, 109, 182; (Loughborough), 109, 182
Hunslet Engine Co, 61, 100, 104, 137, 138, 147, 153; locomotives; 51, 61, 69, 79, 100–1, 102, 103–4, 105, 106, 107–110, 123, 137–9, 141, 145–54, 159, 167–9, 176ff
Hydraulic lifts, 38, 39

Incline carriages, 35, 80–2, 116, 157, 166, 170
Industrial Railway Museum, Penrhyn Castle, 63, 100, 137, 167ff, 175
Industrial Revolution, 11
Ireland, 16, 19, 21, 54, 84, 85

Jung locomotive, 165

Kerr, Stuart & Co, 109; locomotives, 109, 112, 142, 169, 183
Knebworth West Park & Wintergreen Rly, 168

Level crossings, 49, 53, 74, 76, 129, 131ff, 160, 171
Lincolnshire Coast Light Rly, 169
Lister engines, 114, 185; locomotive, 180
Liverpool, 16, 21, 24, 43, 54, 84
Llanberis, 15, 30, 68, 71, 72, 79, 82, 95, 97, 119, 121, 138, 140, 153, 173, 174
Llanberis Lake Rly, 97, 152, 156, 159, 162–5, 166ff, 171, 175, 180
Llanddeiniolen, 17, 20, 131
Llandegai, 17, 34, 41, 44, 45, 54, 57, 74, 101
Llanrwst, 79ff
Llyn Padarn, 17, 21, 68, 71, 72, 74, 79–80, 153, 162, 165
Llyn Peris, 25, 30, 79

# INDEX

Lock-outs, 17, 62, 77, 78; see also Strikes; Unions
Locomotives, see under manufacturer
London, Midland & Scottish Rly, 74, 138
London & North Western Rly, 48, 53, 54, 58, 72, 74, 81, 89, 140, 173
Lytham Motive Power Museum, 167

McAlpine & Sons Ltd, 98, 115
Maenofferen Slate Quarry Co, 110, 111
Maid Marian Locomotive Fund, 152
Manning, Wardle & Co, 110; locomotives, 110, *141*, 169, 183
Marchlyn quarry, 95-7
Marchogion incline, 41
Marinas, 171-2
Menai Bridge, 48, 89
Menai Straits, 13, 17, 18, 54, 56, 83, 91, 172
Midland Rly, 140
Morris, L., 15
Motor Rail locomotives, 163, 164

Nantlle, 11, 13, 14, 77, 93
Nant Peris, 68
Napoleonic Wars, 17, 21, 44, 84
Narrow Gauge Railway Museum, Towyn, 103, 110, 150, 167ff
National Museum of Wales, 166
National Trust, 63
North Wales Quarrying Museum, 97, 165-6, 170
North Wales Quarrymen's Union, 76
North Wales Slate Proprietors' Association, 92, 93

Office level, 38
Ogwen Bank, 41, 43, 61
Oil-firing, 138, 149, 168
Orenstein & Koppel locomotive, 111, *142*, 169, 183

Parliament, 16, 45
Parry, R., 48, 108
Pen Garret gallery, 150ff
Penllyn, 51, 71, 74, 125, 127, 132, 160, 164, 165, 171
Pennant, J., 15; R., 15ff, 23, 41, 43, 54, 56, 173; T., 17

Penrhydd Bach gallery, 151
Penrhyn Castle, 13, 41, 45, 57, 61, 63, 100, 107, 116, 137, 143, 167ff, 175
Penrhyn estate, 13-15, 28, 44ff; park, 13, 41, 57
Penrhyn Quarries Ltd, 63
Penrhyn Sidings, 57, 58
Penscoins, 52, 76, 81, 86, 95, 125, 127, 128, 138, *159*, *160*, 171
Pitt, W., 19
Pittrail Ltd, 95, 139
Pontrhythallt, 71, 74, 125, 127, *160*
Port Dinorwic branch, 84, 89, 90, 173, 174; incline, 68, 72, 76, 81, 85-6, 89, 90 *106*, 128, 174
Port Dinorwic Dry Dock Co, 91
Portmadoc, 84
Port Penrhyn branch, 56-8, 173ff
Port Siding, 89
Porter, A. L., 97, 162, 164
Preservation societies, 63-4, 97
Preserved locomotives, 166-70
Preserved rolling stock, 170
Pritchard & Co, 98
Private carriages, Assheton-Smith's, 70, 80, 140, 143, 170, 174; Lord Penrhyn's, 61, 116, 170, 174

Quainton Railway Soc, 167
Quarrymen, 13ff, 28ff, 44ff, 62ff, 76, 91ff, 119ff, 138ff, 173ff
Quarry Proprietors' Association, 92

Rallt incline, see Port Dinorwic incline
Raybourne Marina, 171
Rennie, G. & J., 135
Rheilffordd Llyn Llanberis, see Llanberis Lake Rly
Road transport, 16, 17, 23-4, 35, 40, 42, 96
Romans, 11
Ropeways, 37-8
Royal visits, 32, 35, 61, 79-83, 157
Rushton, Son & Kenyon, 97
Rushton & Hornsby Ltd, 115; locomotives, 115, 163, 168, 170, 180, 185, 186

Saron, 74, 132
Scotland, 84, 85
Shipping, 16, 22, 43, 54, 56, 83ff, 90, 171, 172
Shrewsbury, 17

Signals, 52, 129, 170
Simplex locomotives, 164
Slate beds, 11, 13, 25, 29, 93, 95; imports, 62–3, 85, 91; prices, 17, 22, 27–9, 67, 76, 78, 79; sizes, 27–9; tax, 17, 19–20, 23, 45, 67
Sledges, 23
Smith, J., 18; W., 18
Smith Rodley steam crane, 171
Snowdon Mountain Rly, 91
Snowdonia, 11, 13, 17
Society for the Defence of Slate Quarrymen, 76
South Africa, 92
South America, 92
Spooner, C. E., 47, 48
Stabla, 74, 125, 127
Staffordshire potteries, 43
Strikes, 17, 46, 62; see also Lock-outs; Unions

Talyllyn Rly, 113, 115
Telford, T., 17, 83
Tileworks, 96
Transhipment, 47, 57ff
Transporters, 59, 72, 88, 120, 128, 143, 158, 170
Tredgold, T., 46, 47
Tregarth, 48, 53
Tunnels, 41, 53, 86, 89, 171
Turner, W., 20, 21, 66

Union Foundry, Caernarvon, see De Winton & Co
Unions, 46, 62, 76, 77; see also Lock-outs; Strikes

United States of America, 62, 67, 76, 84, 101, 103, 104, 113, 114, 168ff

Valley Foundry, Holyhead, see Hughes (Holyhead)
Vaynol estate, 15, 17–18; park, 82, 83
Velocipedes, 87, 97, 119, 125, 127, 144, 166, 170
Village Tramway, 33, 65
Vivian, W. W., 80, 120, 121, 127
Von Dechen, 47
Von Oeynhausen, 47

Wagon turntables, 88, 90, 166
Wales Tourist Board, 164
Warburton family, 14, 15; General, 15, 28
Waterwheels, 97, 165
Welsh Highland Rly, 101
West Lancashire Light Rly, 167, 168
Wheelbarrows, 22, 90, 106
William Parry gallery, 38, 103
Williams, Sir R., 14; W., 16
Workshops, 49, 72, 97, 98, 103, 107, 109, 114, 143, 145, 148, 164, 165
World War I, 27, 62, 85, 86, 92, 93, 101, 131, 153
World War II, 63, 93
Worthington & Co, 43
Wright, S., 15
Wyatt, B., 16, 24, 40, 45; Colonel, 77; J., 56

Yonge family, 14, 15